Key to Cover Illustrations

Accountant/ Retailer/ Sales Agent	Announcer/ Auctioneer	Business Person/ Marketing Expert/ Researcher	Bookseller/ Librarian/ Museum Curator/ Writer
Lab Technician/ Veterinary Technician	Clocker/ Trainer	Architect/ Barn Builder/ Contractor	Farrier
Horse Dentist	Artist/ Illustrator	Photographer	Camp Director/ Riding Instructor/ Saddler
Humane Investigator	Exercise Rider/ Jockey	Veterinarian	Farm Manager/ Wrangler

50 Careers with Horses!

50 CAREERS WITH HORSES!

FROM ACCOUNTANT TO WRANGLER

Bonnie Kreitler

Breakthrough

To Mom and Dad
who finally understood
and bought me a horse

For information, address:
Breakthrough Publications
310 North Highland Avenue
Ossining, New York 10562
www.booksonhorses.com

Manufactured in the United States of America

Library of Congress Catalog Number: 95-077486

ISBN: 0-914327-60-7

Book interior designed by Greenboam & Company

Illustrations by Tricia Tanassy

03 02 01 00 99 98   9 8 7 6 5 4

Acknowledgments

No one writes a book alone. As with all other endeavors in life, we stand on the shoulders of others to reach our goals. It is impossible to thank individually the hundreds of horsemen I have met in over a decade of equine journalism and whose views have found their way into this book. Dozens of these people patiently filled out the career surveys which formed the basis of Chapter 7, generously sharing their experience and knowledge. I hope they will all recognize their contributions and realize the difference their advice may make to the next generation of horse-men-in-training.

Most of the people who grew up when horse transportation was still central to everyday life are gone now. I had the privilege of knowing or interviewing a few of them, including Marvin Drake, Chuck Grant, Charles Kellogg, and Barbara Brewster Taylor, whose invaluable perspective on the evolution of the horse industry is incorporated into Chapter 1. Others still living may recognize their influence here as well. I am grateful for the common-sense economic insights on trends in the horse industry that Clinton Depew, Ph.D., of Louisiana State University, has always been willing to share.

Encouragement to produce a practical career book for horse-loving youth has come from many people. I would be remiss if I did not thank the many people at breed associations, sports associations, and educational institutions who responded cheerfully to requests for information. They all made the job a bit easier. I would like to give special thanks to Dr. Sue Stuska of Martin Community College for permission to quote from her equine education studies. Kirsten Glass and Anita Griswold helped collect and compile survey data and keep the book on schedule. My long-suffering husband (who still wistfully dreams I will outgrow this horse thing someday) and my sons Paul and Charlie also deserve thanks for help with manuscript preparation, taking up a lot of slack, and providing support while this book was aborning.

Last, but certainly far from least, I must acknowledge the late Dorothy Colburn and the late Barbara Brewster Taylor, who both unselfishly responded to another human being's horse-crazed state as though it was the most normal psychosis in all the world. If it were not for their encouragement over the years, this book would not exist. May we all follow in their footsteps.

—Bonnie Kreitler

If a man loves the labor of his trade
apart from any question of success or fame,
the gods have called him.

Robert Lewis Stevenson

Contents

Chapter 1

The Horse Industry

Many horse industry practices and traditions go back a hundred years or more. We still pick out horses' feet every day to ward off thrush, manage our feeding practices to avoid colic, and keep our tack clean to prevent skin galls the same way great-great-grandpa did. Some things never change.

The roles horses play in our society, however, have changed enormously since our ancestors depended on them. Understanding how changes in economics, demographics, and social attitudes affected horses is the first step in anticipating how horses will be used in the twenty-first century so you can prepare for a lifetime of job opportunities.

THE GOLDEN AGE

The Victorian era at the end of the nineteenth century was the heyday of the horse in the United States. Agriculture was booming, America was expanding westward, commerce was booming, and a steadily increasing demand for horses and mules raised both their numbers and their value. There are some interesting parallels between the end of the nineteenth century and the end of the twentieth.

Urban demand for stylish coach and carriage horses during this period made European breeds fashionable. The numbers of Hackneys, Cleveland Bays, and other coaching breeds soared as farmers crossed imported stallions with their draft-type mares to produce more refined animals that fetched good prices in city markets. The German, Hanoverian, and Oldenberg Coach Horse Association of America established its offices in Lafayette, Indiana, while in Chicago the French Coach Horse Society moved in with the American Percheron Horse Breeders Association.

Concurrent with this fad for imported horseflesh, the women's suffrage movement was getting up steam. As they agitated for equal rights for themselves, women also stumped for animal rights, and societies for animal welfare sprang up. Free-thinking homeopathic practitioner Mary Ida Stephanson Young Norton Alexander Denault, for example, developed the formula for Absorbine horse liniment, which her first husband, Wilbur Young, peddled from the back of a wagon. She wanted an alternative to the harsh blisters and concoctions used by horsemen of the day and went on to found the Massachusetts Society for the Prevention of Cruelty to Animals.

Photo courtesy of Ossining Historical Society, Ossining, New York

Main Street traffic in Smalltown, USA, was far from "ONE WAY" in the 1870s .

Women like Mary Ida succeeded in getting American society to see horses as sentient creatures rather than just so much muscle for man's mechanical ends. They also supported and encouraged a growing number of elite events, like New York City's National Horse Show, catering to society horsemen. Farmers had long had agricultural fairs where they could compete with the best of their horses. Now urban horsemen began competitions for their fancy coach horses and gaited saddle horses.

Horsepower had real meaning as the twentieth century dawned. Horses still provided the muscle that sustained commerce, agriculture, and military strength. In *The Horse In America*, Robert West Howard notes that while the human

The James Rowe Wagon dealership, in Ossining, New York

population of the U.S. increased 21 percent from 1900 to 1910, the equine population rose a whopping 70 percent. When World War I began, America had more than 24 million horses and 4.5 million mules, more than the combined horse population of Europe. Even though the Army shipped more than a million horses and mules overseas for the war effort, the loss made hardly a dent in the home population. Census of Agriculture figures show that horses on farms reached an all-time high of 21.5 million in 1918, and that count did not include urban equines.

BETWEEN THE WARS

The end of the horse's heyday was in sight, however. Good riddance, said Henry Ford, who boasted that his gasoline engines would free city dwellers from pollution—no more wet manure underfoot or dried manure blowing in their faces. Thanks to the Federal Highway Act of 1916, some 50,000 miles of roads were improved for car travel between 1917 and 1925, and more Americans traded their horse and carriage for a flivver. The war years had been a boon to agricultural producers, who now had the money to buy Henry Ford's affordable Fordson Tractor.

In 1912, the Census counted 9,000 tractors on American farms. In 1918, Ford sold 133,000 of his new tractors to farmers eager to trade feeding and mucking for an engine that cranked and never kicked. Voices from all sides urged farmers to get rid of horses that were eating grain and grass that could feed humans and meat animals. By 1929, there were more than a million tractors, and draft horses disappeared at the rate of 500,000 per year. When the 1954 Census of Agriculture was concluded, the government announced that, for the first time since they had started counting in 1840, tractors outnumbered horses on farms.

Government support of light horses helped keep overall horse numbers from dwindling even faster. Although the introduction of motorized vehicles in World War I presaged the end for the horse cavalry, the U.S. Army continued to mount cavalry units for another three decades. In 1921, the Army inaugurated an Army Remount Breeding Plan to encourage farmers and ranchers to produce quality animals as potential cavalry mounts. High caliber stallions stood at bargain basement stud fees at a system of Remount Stations throughout the country. Between 600 and 700 stallions sired 9,000 to 10,000 foals annually throughout the 1930s.

Although the Cavalry School at Fort Riley, Kansas, continued teaching recruits throughout World War II and horses saw battlefield action during that conflict (the last mounted U.S. Cavalry action against an enemy force occurred on the Philippine island of Luzon when the 26th Cavalry was annihilated in an engagement with the Japanese), horses had not really been vital to national defense since World War I. The United States Army officially disbanded its horse cavalry in 1948 after fielding the final U.S. military team to compete in the Olympics.

Another federal government effort on behalf of light horses was launched at the turn of the century, when the U.S. Department of Agriculture stepped in to pull the American Morgan horse breed back from the brink. Horsemen who were concerned because crossbreeding with other breeds had almost obliterated original Morgan blood had implored the U.S Department of Agriculture for help in saving the breed. In 1905, the department's experiment station in Burlington, Vermont, advertised for Morgan mares to begin an effort to save the old Morgan type. And in 1907, Colonel Joseph Battell donated a farm in Weybridge, Vermont, to the government for the purpose of preserving the Morgan horse. The USDA maintained the Morgan breeding project for almost 50 years, with some of the stallions being used in the Army remount program and in another program to provide quality horses to Indian reservations. The government voted to discontinue the project in 1950 and the Vermont legislature voted to take over the farm to be run by its College of Agriculture.

Throughout the years following World War I and the Great Depression, when overall horse numbers were declining, people still enjoyed watching a good horse race. When Harry Straus's American Totalisator Co., Inc., installed the first tote board at Arlington Park Race Track outside Chicago in 1933, it signaled the beginning of new government support. This time, it was state support of the racing industry. With Straus's invention to make the system of laying bets, giving odds, and figuring payouts uniform and fair, state governments found racetracks and the revenues from pari-mutuel betting an economically attractive segment of the horse industry to be supported and encouraged.

Mechanization never made significant inroads against

Courtesy of Virginia Polytechnic Institute and State University, Shenandoah Valley Agricultural Research and Extension Center, McCormick Farm

Tractors threw thousands of horses —and the service industries that supported them—out of work in the 1930s and 1940s.

horsepower and horse sense west of the Mississippi, where cowboys and ranchers plied their trade. Texas consistently led the nation in horse population numbers. In 1940, a group of Texas horsemen met in Eagle Pass to found the American Quarter Horse Association and begin registering horses in what would become the world's most populous breed by the end of the century.

Throughout the 1930s, 40s, and 50s, wealthier families who could afford to keep horses for recreation and less affluent but die-hard horsemen continued to fox hunt, play polo, and show their horses. Large stables in urban areas catered to those who still loved the horse. The late Chuck Grant recounted his days as a riding instructor in the late 1930s at a riding academy in the heart of downtown Chicago that maintained 100 school horses. Night classes drew up to 75 riders who rode four abreast, head-to-tail in

POPULATION TRENDS

Based on data from the U. S. Census Bureau, the American Horse Council,
the American Veterinary Medical Association,
breed associations, and other miscellaneous sources

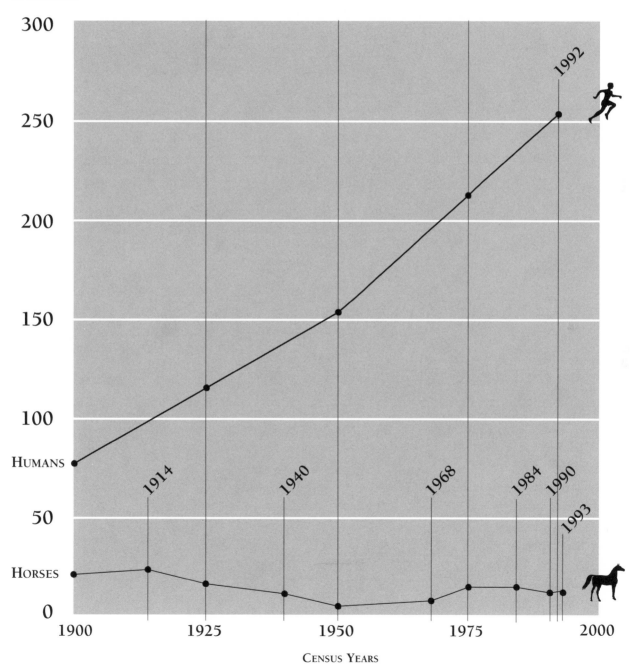

THE TEN HORSIEST STATES

Based on horse population estimates in the
American Horse Council's 1985 National Equine Survey

#1 Texas
#2 California
#3 Oklahoma
#4 Colorado
#5 New York
#6 Ohio
#7 Michigan
#8 Pennsylvania
#9 Washington
#10 Kentucky

a small indoor arena. Saturdays and Sundays began with breakfast rides of up to 300 horses through nearby Lincoln Park. Similar scenes played out in Washington, D.C.'s Rock Creek Park and in New York City's Central Park, where social swells during the golden age had "taken the air" in their carriages.

In 1917, a group of wealthy sportsmen and equestrian patrons led by Reginald C. Vanderbilt had founded the Association of American Horse Shows (now the American Horse Shows Association) to set uniform rules for fair competition at society horse shows. In 1935, the AHSA took over the U.S. membership in the Federation Equestrian Internationale from the Cavalry Association. When the Army bowed out of international competition in 1948, AHSA-member sportsmen banded together to found, finance, and loan horses to a civilian United States Equestrian Team. Affirming the belief of those horsemen that horse sports could survive without government subsidy, the first civilian USET team fielded at the 1952 Helsinki Olympics came home with two bronze medals.

To the amazement of many who thought that horses would eventually fade away, horse numbers rebounded dramatically after World War II. Post-war prosperity resulted in a growing middle class with greater leisure time. Horses were no longer just the province of the affluent or those with agricultural roots. Greater leisure time made it possible for more people to own horses for recreation.

THE SECOND HALF-CENTURY

Significantly, a group of children who came to be known as the "baby boomers" were moving through the population pipeline at mid-century. As these children passed through pre-adolescence, many of them wanted to ride. Then they wanted a horse of their own. Since the Census of Agriculture counted only horses on farms and not those kept in cities or suburbs for pleasure riding or show, accurate figures on total horse numbers at mid-century are hard to find. Registration numbers for purebred horses, however, began showing an encouraging trend. Between 1960 and 1968, new registrations more than doubled. They more than doubled again by 1982. As light horse numbers boomed, so did a demand for riding stables, riding instructors, and other services. A pleasure horse market emerged that was larger, stronger, and

AMERICA'S MOST POPULAR BREEDS

*Breeds reporting 10,000 or more total animals registered
according to the 1994 and 1995 volumes of the Horse Industry Directory
(American Horse Council, Washington, D.C.)*

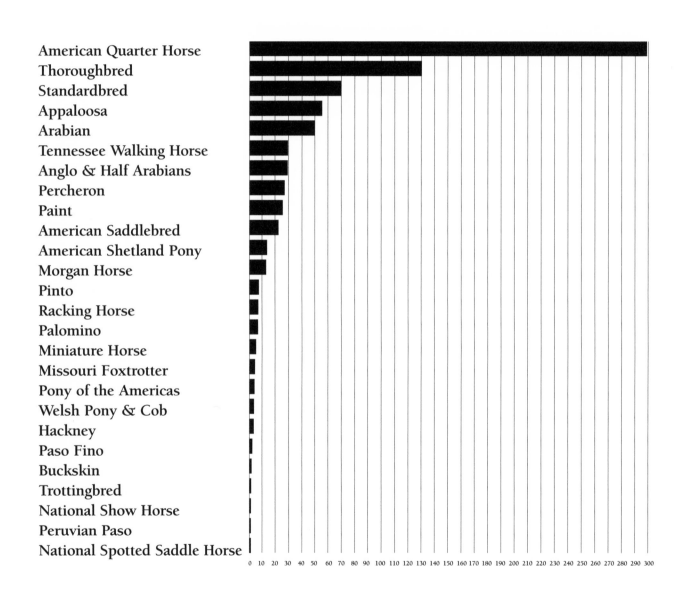

American Quarter Horse	
Thoroughbred	
Standardbred	
Appaloosa	
Arabian	
Tennessee Walking Horse	
Anglo & Half Arabians	
Percheron	
Paint	
American Saddlebred	
American Shetland Pony	
Morgan Horse	
Pinto	
Racking Horse	
Palomino	
Miniature Horse	
Missouri Foxtrotter	
Pony of the Americas	
Welsh Pony & Cob	
Hackney	
Paso Fino	
Buckskin	
Trottingbred	
National Show Horse	
Peruvian Paso	
National Spotted Saddle Horse	

0 10 20 30 40 50 60 70 80 90 100 110 120 130 140 150 160 170 180 190 200 210 220 230 240 250 260 270 280 290 300

NUMBERS IN TEN THOUSANDS

more broadly based than any previous market for cavalry horses, draft horses, show horses, or race horses.

Other trends shaped up in the horse industry in the late 1950s and 1960s. Automobile engines were now strong enough to pull weight like a good draft horse and clever horsemen began designing and building wheeled boxes to haul their horses longer distances than they could ride them. Personal horse trailers provided the mobility that helped fuel a boom in horse shows. To compete with their horses, riders no longer had to wait for the agricultural fair circuit to begin in summer or have access to the society horse shows on the East Coast and in major cities. Smaller shows for anybody who could get there mushroomed nationwide. By 1994, the American Horse Council counted 14,000 shows sanctioned by major associations such as the AHSA and the AQHA and estimated there were thousands more unsanctioned shows nationwide.

The increase in horses fueled an increase in the things people wanted to do with them, from cutting to dressage. The horse shows that included several breeds and riding disciplines in the late 1950s into the early 1970s gave way to shows devoted to one breed or a single sports discipline. As competition grew keener and trainers began specializing, horse shows evolved into single breed or single discipline events. Mega-events like the annual Quarter Horse Congress in Columbus, Ohio, began drawing entries from all over the country for competitions lasting a week or more. Those post-war backyard horse shows grew into a major new segment in the horse industry.

Light horse numbers rose steadily into the mid-1980s. Then came a double economic whammy. The first blow was a nationwide economic recession that began in the 1970s. It slowed the surging growth rate of the 60s and 70s and began wringing horses out of many middle-class budgets. Breeders of high-caliber horses fared better than those producing average-grade horses, but at all levels, breeders stopped breeding mares and culled their broodmare bands as they found they could not sell young stock without taking a loss.

The second blow was a 1986 change in the tax laws that made it more difficult to deduct losses from horse activities against income earned from non-horse sources. That change, combined with a loss of overseas buyers due to the world economic situation, hit the racing industry hard and yearling auction prices plummeted. It also squeezed many "gentleman breeders"

out of the light horse business. Purebred registration figures
peaked in 1984 then began dropping steadily back to mid-1970s
levels. Between 1984 and 1990, total new registrations dropped
off 25 percent. The precipitous decline slowed in the early 1990s,
with recreational breeds such as the Quarter Horse, Paint, and
Morgan and Saddlebreds showing small increases in 1993-94
registration figures, indicating renewed optimism on the part of
breeders.

THE HORSE INDUSTRY OF THE FUTURE

The successful job seeker in the horse industry of the twenty-first
century needs to keep in mind who the horse industry's clientele
are going to be and whether they deal with those clients directly
as a business owner or indirectly as someone working for a horse-
related business.

The lesson from the 1970s and 1980s is that horse numbers
and activities are more sensitive to shifts in the national economy
than many horsemen understood, and the horse industry seems
to take several years to fully react to major new pressures. Data
gathered by various breed and sport associations indicate that the
typical horse owner is no longer a farmer or a wealthy sportsman
but a solidly middle-class young adult or middle-aged married
American with an annual income between $40,000 to $70,000
and owning from one to five horses, usually kept at home. The
horse industry needs to find ways to emphasize that horses are no
longer just for wealthy people if the industry's base is to expand in
the future. Casting off the elite image left over from the 1930s and
l940s will be the job of equine marketers and journalists.

Although gender ratios vary from breed to breed and sport to
sport, horse owners are predominantly female. While a sizable
number of those females are teenagers, a high percentage of them
are also middle-aged baby boomers. One factor in the growth of
dressage riding appears to be aging baby boomer riders who have
decided their jumping days are behind them. If these riders
choose to continue owning horses as they become card-carrying
senior citizens, breeders of easy-gaited horses or trainers of driving
horses may also find new customers.

Many trainers comment that another old pattern seems to be
changing. Previously, teenagers rode and competed actively until
college, family formation, or career building pushed horses out of

their lives, at least temporarily. More and more of these young adults are finding ways to continue their horse activities, however. That means a growing demand for adult amateur classes at horse shows and for different patterns of training and horse ownership that can co-exist with the pressures of career building, setting up house, and starting a family.

Meanwhile, demographers are taking note of a new baby "boomlet." The baby boomers had children, and the first of those children are beginning to form their own families. The result is a birth bulge that, although not as large as that in the late 1940s and early 1950s, promises to give school officials, day-care operators, and diaper manufacturers a lot of business. If the horse industry does its promotion homework, those children will also give new business to riding instructors, lesson stables, horse shows, clothing manufacturers and others. However, horsemen will not be competing with other breeds or riding disciplines for the attention of this new generation. They will compete with baseball teams, soccer leagues, ballet schools, and swim teams.

The horse industry as it approaches the twenty-first century is becoming more global. Racing enthusiasts were the first to embrace air travel for their horses, then horse show competitors. Now, like those Victorian coaching enthusiasts who hankered after European horseflesh, even recreational riders shop overseas for a sporthorse. Meanwhile, Europeans and Asians are buying into Quarter Horses and the American cowboy image. This will create new international opportunities in sales of not only horses but also Western tack and clothing. One employment agency specializing in the horse industry reports a new opportunity: requests from overseas clients for English-speaking riding instructors and trainers.

Just as the horse industry in the first half of the century was pressured by the rising use of the gasoline-powered engine, the

As long as there are horses, there will be a need for the work and tools of the farrier.

horse industry in the first half of the twenty-first century must face and deal with pressures that could restrict industry growth. On the other hand, meeting each of these challenges offers an opportunity for new direction and new jobs.

Primary among these pressures is the loss of agricultural lands to development at the fringes of our urban areas. High land costs, property taxes, and restrictive zoning make it more difficult for people to own and use horses in places close to good jobs with incomes that make horses affordable. Creeping urbanization eats up trails and open spaces for riding as well as paddocks and pastures. Horsemen will need to find ways to cooperate with other recreational groups that also want to use available trails and open space and find creative ways to increase riding options in trailless areas. Equine-oriented recreation specialists can lead this effort.

As the horse population gets pushed farther away from cities and suburbs, those who would like to ride occasionally must travel farther to reach places where they can ride. There are also fewer places offering trail rides and riding lessons because the threat of lawsuits and skyrocketing insurance premiums have pushed many hack stables out of business and forced other stables to drop their lesson programs. Loss of these recreational opportunities denies the horse industry dollars from literally millions of people who would choose to ride occasionally if it were convenient. Alternate recreation opportunities from boating and skiing to golf and tennis will compete even more intensely for recreation dollars and time in the future than they do now.

The horseman who figures out how to provide riding opportunities and horse experiences in a setting reasonably close to urban dwellers will be in demand. Many states have taken the first step to help them by passing laws that limit the liability of equine professionals such as riding stable operators and dude ranch operators. Event organizer Joy Meierhans proved that horses still have enormous appeal to a large segment of the general population when she mounted the first multi-day horse festival at Arlington Park Racetrack outside Chicago in the late 1980s. Other equine entrepreneurs followed suit with large regional horse fairs at Belmont Park in New York City and other locations. Dinner theaters featuring horse entertainment in Florida and Illinois are another example. Some industry watchers feel that the best salaries in the horse industry will be available in horse operations like these that bring outside money into the industry.

Women are an important market for the horse industry, but

many horse businesses still operate in the same way they did thirty or forty years ago when most women were stay-at-home mothers with daytime hours available to ride. Over half of American women now work outside the home and that percentage continues to rise. That growing number of working women has greater disposable income than ever before but they have less time. Without evening and weekend programs, they will not be able to ride and spend that money on horses. Many women also worry about the time commitment required by full horse ownership and how they can juggle work, horses, and families. Equine entrepreneurs who develop creative leasing, horse sharing arrangements, or riding co-ops can benefit handsomely by tapping this market.

One Massachusetts stable has already anticipated the twenty-first century with an evening and weekend program that combines riding with stretching and aerobics for working women. Horsemen who break out of the old patterns to develop creative lesson packages like this, leasing programs, private clubs with members sharing groups of horses, or barns where boarders share in chores to keep costs down will find customers.

Dependent on pari-mutuel betting for much of its cash flow, the racing industry is under tremendous competitive pressure from newer forms of legalized gambling including state lotteries, off-track betting, and casinos on Indian reservations. As betting takes go down, so do purses and the incomes of trainers and everyone else on the shedrow whose salary is dependent on them. How the Thoroughbred industry addresses those challenges will have an impact on the large number of horse-related jobs in that industry.

Horsemen in the twenty-first century will also have to deal with pressures from environmentalists demanding changes in standard horse-keeping practices and restrictions on trail and back country access. Animal rights activists have vowed to end horse ownership and other uses of horses. Like other pressures on the horse industry, meeting these challenges can create new job opportunities that did not exist even a few years ago.

Many horse-industry career choice decisions are made with the heart and passion that is an essential ingredient for success in any field. By using your head as well as your heart to analyze which segments of the horse industry are growing, changing, holding steady, or shrinking, you can improve the odds of finding a career that you love in a part of the industry that will still be thriving when you begin contemplating retirement.

CAREER CLOSE-UP

VETERINARY TECHNICIAN

Sandy Terceño bends over the desk, carefully matching vials of blood with the proper paperwork before they go to the state lab. The job needs to be done before she heads out on her rounds as a veterinary technician with one of the clinic's equine vets, but making sure the job is done correctly has top priority. If a positive test were attributed to the wrong horse, there would be potential for disaster.

As an equine veterinary technician, Sandy is responsible for handling administrative and lab duties so that the veterinarians can leverage their available treatment time. To prepare for her career, she earned a Bachelor's degree in animal science, emphasizing classes that had to do with horses. She studied breeding, anatomy, and physiology, took any hands-on labs offered, and tried to develop as well-rounded a background as possible. After graduation, she looked for jobs related to horses but was unable to find one that paid enough to support both herself and her horse. She settled temporarily for a job as an assistant to a human dentist, which kept her in the medical field. When she heard of an opening as a veterinary technician at a nearby equine clinic, she applied. Her work as a dental assistant was the deciding factor for her new employers because it showed her ability to work well in a supporting role with a medical professional.

Now Sandy checks the schedule for the day and helps the veterinarians set up any supplies they need in advance. "The key is to always be one step ahead of the doctor," she says, efficiently anticipating what he is going to need so that work can progress smoothly. She cites the example of a horse that needs radiographs. Once the vet determines that they should be taken, he might stop to discuss with the horse's owner what the radiographs might show. Meanwhile, Sandy gets the equipment out and ready so that when their discussion is over, the work can proceed quickly. An efficient veterinary technician might enable the veterinarian to schedule several more stops over the course of a day than would be possible if the vet were working alone.

Back at the clinic, the technician can help handle paperwork and restock supplies while the veterinarian returns phone calls and consults with colleagues on perplexing cases. By working as a team, they are able to provide clients with better, faster service.

A veterinary technician must be a flexible person, Sandy notes. There is something new every day, something different every day, and the hours can be irregular in an equine practice. One day, they may finish rounds at 4 p.m., but the next day may stretch well into the evening for a horse that needs critical-care nursing. Some weekends, Sandy wears a beeper so that she can be reached for emergencies, such as colic surgeries. "I like being very busy," she says. Although some veterinary technicians decide to return to school and become licensed veterinarians, Sandy enjoys her supporting role. "I'm paid to do what I love," she says. And helping horses brings her daily satisfaction. ■

Chapter 2

Focusing on a Goal

Looking at the horse industry for areas of future job growth or contraction is just the first step in focusing on a career goal or even on several appealing possibilities. Thinking about things they enjoy doing or things they would like to do is the way many people narrow their career choices. In the horse industry, however, that might not be the most practical approach because jobs that involve working directly with horses have the greatest appeal, and competition for them drives down the income derived from them.

Given their first choice of horse careers, most people would probably opt to become a professional rider, riding instructor, or horse trainer. If everyone got their wish, however, there would not be enough horses or riding students to support all of those riders, instructors, and trainers. They might have a really good time for awhile, but eventually they would all starve because there would not be enough horses and pupils to go around.

So where else do people work in the horse industry? There are many, many more jobs available working indirectly with horses than there are working with them directly on a daily basis. Some of these jobs offer a certain amount of hands-on horse contact, others may offer little or none. All offer an opportunity to be part of the greater horse industry and to enjoy a working relationship with others who love horses.

The total number of horses as we approach the year 2000 is difficult to pin down because no one counts every segment of the horse industry. Extrapolating from data available from the American Horse Council, the American Veterinary Medical Association, and the U.S. Census Bureau, the United States will probably have between ten and eleven million horses as the turn of the century approaches. State and regional studies indicate that there is approximately one horse-related job for every two to three horses, which means there are 3.3 to 5.5 million jobs related to the horse industry in some way.

The following lists are a guide to potential career choices in the horse industry. Some careers—such as being a jockey or a wrangler—require skills unique to a single segment of the horse industry. The skills required for others—such as being an equine veterinarian or a stable manager—can be employed in several segments. Still other careers—such as being a writer or a veterinary technician—call for skills useful both within and outside the horse industry.

A longer list does not necessarily mean that a particular segment of the industry offers more jobs, only a greater variety of them. For example, if there are 179 pari-mutuel racetracks in the country, that means there are only 179 jobs available nationwide as a racetrack manager. If you decide you want to narrow your choice to racetracks that run only Quarter Horses or Paints or Arabians, the number of jobs becomes smaller still. If there are only fifty states, that puts an automatic cap on the number of potential state extension horse specialists (there are actually fewer since not all states hire horse specialists). Looking at it another way, if there are eight million horses that need to be fed, there will be thousands of opportunities in feed sales and handling.

Trainers are needed wherever horses are to be ridden or entered into competition.

JOB OPPORTUNITIES IN THE HORSE INDUSTRY

HORSE RACING

auction clerk
auctioneer
backstretch stable hand
barn foreman
bloodstock agent
breeder
broodmare manager
clerk of scales
clocker
equine appraiser
equine insurance agent
farm exercise rider
farm groom
farm hand
farm manager
foaling attendant
handicapper
harness driver
horse auction manager
hot walker
jockey
jockey's agent

jockey's valet
paddock judge
patrol judge
pedigree researcher/analyst
race starter
racehorse trainer
racetrack manager
racetrack official
racing form publisher
racing form writer
racing chemist
racing secretary
racing steward
stallion manager
state racing commissioner
tattoo inspector
track exercise rider
track groom
track marketing/publicity
track office staff
track photographer

HORSE HEALTH & WELFARE

animal abuse investigator
animal behaviorist
animal ethologist
artificial insemination technician
clinical veterinarian
equine dentist
equine massage therapist
equine nutritionist
equine pharmacologist
equine veterinary acupuncturist
equine veterinary chiropractor
federal animal welfare inspector
federal or state veterinarian
freeze branding technician

humane society manager
humane society staff member
industrial veterinarian
lab technician
microchip implant technician
private practice veterinarian
surgical technician
veterinary office support staff
veterinary technician
X-ray technician

PUREBRED HORSE INDUSTRY

artificial insemination
   technician
association clerical staff
association events coordinator
association manager
association marketing director
association publications editor

blood typing lab technician
breeder
equine insurance agent
pedigree researcher
registry inspector
tattoo or brand inspector

HORSE EVENT INDUSTRY

breeder
equine appraiser
equine insurance agent
equine journalist
event publicist
farm manager
groom
grounds manager
horse sales agent
horse show computer systems
   specialist
horse show course designer
horse show/rodeo announcer
horse show/rodeo arena crew
horse show/rodeo judge

horse show/rodeo manager
horse show/rodeo secretary
horse show steward
horse show videographer
mounted security or
   courtesy patrol
prize list/program ad
   sales rep
prize list/program editor
ribbon/trophy manufacturer
rodeo stock contractor
show horse trainer/clinician
show/rodeo photographer
stable help
trade show organizer

FEED & SUPPLEMENT INDUSTRY

advertising/marketing specialist
commodity trader
corporate financial
   officer/accountant
equine nutritionist
feed chemist
feed formulator
feed mill designer
production engineer
production staff
purchasing agent

quality control staff
regional distributor
regional sales staff
regulatory compliance
   specialist
retail feed store owner
retail store bookkeeper
retail store sales staff
retail store warehouse staff
technical representative

INDUSTRY PROMOTION

equine journalist
trade event publicist

trade show organizer
trade show staff

RESEARCH & EDUCATION

4-H agent	reproductive physiology
animal ethologist	specialist
college-level teaching staff	research chemist
county extension agent	research journal editor
equine nutritionist	research librarian
feed chemist	state extension horse
geneticist	specialist
museum curator	statistician
museum staff	technical school instructor
pharmaceutical chemist	

RECREATION & TOURISM

assistant instructor	horse packing outfitter
barn manager	horse trainer/clinician
boarding stable groom/staff	mounted park ranger
boarding stable manager	park recreation planner
boarding stable owner	polo club manager
camp riding program director	professional "pet sitter"
camp riding program instructor	ranch hand
carriage ride concessionaire	ranch manager
dude ranch operator	riding club manager
dude ranch wrangler	riding instructor
fox hunt huntsman	stable helper
fox hunt kennel help	trail maintenance crew
hack stable operator	travel agent for equestrian
handicapped-program manager	tours
handicapped-riding instructor	

MANUFACTURING (TACK, GROOMING & STABLE EQUIPMENT)

advertising/marketing specialist	purchasing agent
corporate financial	regional sales manager
analyst/accountant	regional sales representative
corporate sales manager	regional wholesale
product developer	distributor
product researcher	technical representative
production line engineer	warehouse manager
production line staff	warehouse packer

EQUINE RETAILING & SERVICES

auction clerk
auction sales organizer
auctioneer
blanket washer and repairer
carriage dealer
carriage restorer
clipper-sharpening service
custom embroiderer
custom engraver
equine book dealer—new or
  antiquarian
feed/farm-supply store
  manager
feed/farm-supply store owner
in-store sales staff
purchasing/bookkeeping staff
saddle or harness maker
sport art or antiques dealer
tack repair and leather worker
tack shop manager
tack shop owner
truck and trailer dealer

JOB OPPORTUNITIES CROSSING ALL INDUSTRY SEGMENTS

accountant for horse businesses
agricultural engineer
architect for horse facilities
barn & arena construction
  contractor
commercial horse hauler
equine advertising copywriter
equine advertising media buyer
equine artist
equine flight attendant
equine insurance sales
equine public relations or
  advertising rep
equine photographer
equine videographer
equine writer
farm fencing contractor
farrier
horse magazine ad sales rep
horse publication art
  director/designer
horse publication circulation
  manager
horse publication editor
horse publication publisher
horse sales agent
lawyer specializing in horses
mounted security officer
real estate agent for horse
  properties
veterinarian
veterinary technician

How do you know what skills you'll need for the careers that appeal to you? For some careers, such as becoming a veterinarian, those skills may be obvious. A little simple research can help with others. If there is an association of people working in that career, write to see if they offer career materials and ask for the name of someone working in the field who would be willing to discuss their work with you. The addresses for many of these associations are included in the descriptions of specific careers in Chapter 7. You can also consult the list of associations in the American Horse Council's annual *Horse Industry Directory* (1700 K

Street N.W., Washington, D.C. 20006; 202-296-4031; $20 or free to members). Ask among fellow horsemen or at tack and feed stores to locate someone in the field. Write the American Horse Council's American Youth Horse Council (4193 Iron Works Pike, Lexington, KY 40511-2742) and ask them to supply the name of a working professional. Contact the placement office at a college or university offering courses that prepare people for your target career, and ask for the names of some recent graduates. Add to your list the name of at least one person or company that might hire someone for a particular career.

Compile a list of at least two or three people to contact. Write, call, or set up an appointment to visit these people. Ask someone who hires people in that career what qualities they look for when hiring and what skills they expect that person to have. Ask people working in the career what skills they see as essential to do their job. Discuss how you can get those skills. Are they skills that can be learned only through hands-on experience, through education, or through a combination of the two?

EDUCATION VS. EXPERIENCE

There has long been a debate in the horse industry over which is more important: education or experience. There is no simple answer. Any response has to be qualified several ways.

First, what skills does the job require and how are they best obtained? It is obvious that veterinarians, university instructors, scientists, and lawyers need college-level instruction to prepare for their professions. On-the-job experience is not sufficient preparation for careers in these fields.

The education vs. experience debate is not so clear cut when it comes to working directly with horses on a daily basis. Here, there is general industry-wide agreement that there is no teacher like experience and you can never have enough of it. No matter how long you have worked with horses, there is always one out there waiting to teach you something you didn't know. The person who has grown up with horses and has thousands of hours of hands-on experience has a hard-to-beat edge over the job candidate whose horse experience amounts to a few years of riding lessons or even a two-year college program in equine studies.

Does that mean college-level training is useless if you want a hands-on horse career? No, only that any two- or four-year program must be carefully evaluated in relationship to your long-term career goals. Some programs concentrate on riding and the skills necessary to become a riding instructor or coach. Others focus on horse care or farm management. If a program does not offer training in the skills you need for your career choice, the certificate or degree may *not* be much value in achieving your goals.

There is also a hard fact of life in the horse industry that you will not hear about from the admissions offices of schools offering equine studies programs. Many old hands in the horse industry are quite outspoken that they are unimpressed by diplomas, certificates, or any other piece of paper. In fact, some actually view a certificate or degree in equine studies as a negative factor in hiring. The people enrolled in these programs often have minimal horse experience going in, these older horsemen point out. Some courses offer mostly classroom theory and not enough hands-on practice. Yet the graduates appear at the barn door, resumes in hand, cocksure of themselves and what they think they know. They have difficulty accepting that the instructor or trainer's way of doing something may be different from what they were taught in school. Interpersonal friction and job dissatisfaction are so common that these old hands are often gun shy about hiring people with degrees.

On the other side are horsemen with a different perspective of the horse industry. They feel that college-educated employees have valuable skills to offer to their businesses. While solid horse-care skills are still important, these horsemen also recognize that college-educated employees have better communication skills, greater poise and maturity in dealing with clients, and an understanding of business principles, which makes them valuable team players. In recent years, many equine studies programs have beefed up their business offerings to meet the needs of these modern horsemen and better prepare their graduates for careers. Note a telling point here: It is the graduate's *non*-horse skills these potential employers find attractive, skills that can be acquired only through education.

It is also very important to remember that attitudes, appearance, and work habits can be just as important to employers as your experience and education. Horse industry employment services report that when they ask employers what they are looking for in an employee, non-horse skills are mentioned in almost the same breath as horse skills. Loyalty, reliability, promptness, neatness, and other traits are highly valued by employers whose business may depend on how their employees treat clients. Dr. Sue Stuska, head of the equine technologies department at Martin Community College in Williamston, North Carolina, used software developed by Daniel Vogler of Virginia Polytechnic Institute and State University to rank a list of 613 things that a student in a two-year equine studies program might learn according to their importance to horse industry employers. Employers ranked each skill as *essential, expected, nice to have,* or *low priority.* Stuska found that 417 of the learning targets fell into the employers' ESSENTIAL or EXPECTED rankings and 18 percent of those were categorized as "attitudes" rather than as knowledge or motor skills.

A good show groom can mean the difference between success and failure when campaigning the horse.

If your long-term career goals are extremely modest, experience alone may be the only qualification you need for jobs such as a groom, exercise rider, or tack shop sales staff. However, if you plan to use these entry-level jobs as a stepping stone to jobs with greater responsibility, adding education and skills beyond horse care to your resume can only help. The most commonly cited advice from established horsemen to those aspiring to upper-level careers with horses is to get as much education as possible before setting off to find that first job. That, they say, is the best way to open the widest possible range of options and insure adequate lifetime earning power.

WORKING CONDITIONS

Besides thinking about the skills your career choices require and how to acquire them, you need to consider the working conditions you enjoy. When you call the people on your contacts list to learn more about skills, education, and experience, ask about working conditions in the field, too.

Some horse careers keep people outdoors a high percentage of the time regardless of season or weather, either with or without direct contact with horses. Horse trainers, farriers, barn builders, fencing contractors, and mounted policemen spend a high percentage of their time outdoors. Other careers are primarily indoor occupations. Blood-typing chemists and editors for horse publications, for example, spend most of their time indoors.

A fair number of horse industry careers offer a blend of indoor and outdoor activity. Equine veterinarians may be outdoors while visiting clients but they also work indoors making necessary phone calls, keeping up their practice's records, checking their inventory of medications, keeping current on the newest treatments and procedures reported in journals and at conferences, and doing surgery. Even farm managers and riding instructors who spend the majority of their time outdoors (which includes barns and indoor arenas) must spend a certain amount of time behind a desk keeping records, sending out billings, and organizing their marketing efforts.

Required working hours may be very important in making a career choice. Horses must be fed and cared for seven days a week, rain or shine, in blistering heat or bitter cold. They often have an uncanny way of getting into trouble and needing veterinary attention at inconvenient hours. Foaling season means nights without sleep. Show season can mean 18-hour workdays that start with mane braiding or a trailer ride at 4 a.m. and are not over until 10 p.m. that night. The person who grumbles when the workday gets longer than eight hours need not apply.

There are horse-related jobs, however, that offer fairly regular hours. If you are a person who likes predictability—likes to be able to plan when you will have the time to ride your own horse or schedule a vacation or needs to fit a job around the demands of a family—jobs in areas like association work, manufacturing, or retailing might be better job choices than being a broodmare manager or a veterinary technician.

Climbing a career ladder in the horse industry frequently

requires mobility. Racetrack personnel live a gypsy life as they move from track to track. At the upper levels of the horse show circuit, trainers and their personnel are on the move from weekend to weekend during the season. If you don't like living out of a suitcase or eating a lot of fast food, look at a different job option

Some segments of the horse industry are strongly oriented to one region or another. Florida, California, Kentucky, and New York are likely destinations for anyone who wants to work in the Thoroughbred industry, for example. If you specialize in Spanish horses like Peruvian Paso or Paso Fino, the greatest number of job opportunities will be in Florida, California, and Texas. If you are focusing on a particular segment of the horse industry, you need to be aware of these geographic patterns when you ultimately go looking for a job. Again, this is something to question the people on your contact list about.

Mobility is also important if you plan to climb many career ladders because so many horse-related businesses are very small. Job openings that allow you to move up in responsibility and pay may occur so infrequently that moving ahead within a given company or association is difficult. To move up, you may have to pack up and move out as positions become available in other organizations. One professional offers the example of a Thoroughbred broodmare farm with thirty or forty employees. A groom there might aspire to become head groom, but to climb the career ladder still farther and become a stable manager or foreman, he would have to leave that employer and go elsewhere. Not only is there only one position he could hope to fill, but many farm owners also prefer to go outside to hire foremen who already have management experience.

Some people like the security of knowing exactly what they are to do and how to do it. They prefer carrying out decisions that other people have made. Their employers probably prefer people who do exactly as they are told without questioning or debating alternatives. Other people thrive on responsibility. They love solving problems, taking on and learning a job they have never done before, and running the show. Their employers probably prefer delegating authority so they can attend to other business. Knowing your own personal work style and meshing it with the management style of your employer are key to satisfaction on both sides.

The ultimate degree of responsibility is running your own business. Those running a business trade a steady paycheck for

WORKING CONDITIONS CHECKLIST

Consider which of the job traits below are most appealing to you;
then compare your choices against the career-by-career information
on working conditions in Chapter 7.

Contact With Horses
_____ a. I want to work directly with horses on a daily basis.

_____ b. I would be satisfied working directly with horses occasionally.

_____ c. Direct on-the-job contact is not essential.

Place of Work
_____ a. I prefer working outdoors (which includes barns and indoor arenas).

_____ b. I prefer working indoors.

_____ c. I would like a job that provides a mix of indoor and outdoor activities.

Working Hours
_____ a. I do not mind working irregular hours, including evenings and weekends, without overtime pay.

_____ b. I prefer predictable hours and would expect overtime pay for extra work time.

Travel and Relocation
_____ a. I would enjoy a job that required frequent travel.

_____ b. I would find frequent travel inconvenient.

_____ c. I can easily relocate, even several times, to move up a career ladder.

_____ d. Relocating would be difficult for me.

Responsibility Levels and Risk
_____ a. I like being told exactly what I am to do.

_____ b. I like solving problems on my own.

_____ c. I prefer a set list of job duties.

_____ d. I enjoy flexibility and sharing a variety of duties.

_____ e. I prefer not to make major decisions.

_____ f. I enjoy being given new responsibilities.

_____ g. I like the predictability of a regular paycheck.

_____ h. I can manage my budget with an irregular cash flow.

_____ i. I am willing to risk money starting my own business.

_____ j. I am not willing to risk any money to reach my career goals.

complete personal autonomy. Being your own boss can be very appealing but it means very careful planning to ensure that the business can generate sufficient income to succeed. Starting up means investing money—your own or that of others—which you may lose if your planning is inadequate or based on poor business assumptions. There are many jobs in the horse industry, however, that are really small businesses. Farriers, horse dentists, tack shop owners, many veterinarians, and others have all invested capital in equipment and inventory. In addition to their horse-specific skills, they also need business and management skills to succeed.

Many people start off thinking about a career in the horse industry with a rather vague notion that they want to "work with horses." Their emotional attachment to these beautiful, powerful, yet often delicate creatures is so strong that they are willing to do any job, anywhere, in order to be close to them. And everyone, of course, wants to ride.

The result is a glut of people competing for entry-level jobs such as grooms, assistant trainers, and assistant riding instructors, or other jobs working directly with horses. That intense competition for a fairly limited number of positions means low wages that are often not even enough to completely support the employee much less any horse he or she might own. It also means fast burnout and quick turnover in many of these jobs.

If you study the lists of horse industry jobs, it should quickly be evident that there are far more jobs, often at better pay, for people willing to work indirectly with horses at many levels in the industry. As you think about career choices, think in terms of career ladders or tracks. Will your initial career choice lead to greater responsibility, income, and other job possibilities in the future? Ask the people on your contacts lists where they think they will be in ten years if they stay in the field.

A carefully considered starting career choice can begin a rewarding lifetime of work in the horse industry. An impulsive or poor decision may mean that, for lack of opportunity or income stagnation, at some point you will be forced to leave the horse industry to work elsewhere only to find you lack skills transferable to other jobs.

A COMFORTABLE INCOME

Determining what you consider a comfortable income is another important part of your career planning. *Comfortable* means sufficient income to meet your wants and needs without necessarily putting you in the lap of luxury. *Comfortable* will be different things for different people. An income that one person may consider affluent might seem like borderline poverty to another. *Comfortable* might include the ability to own and maintain a horse (but remember, you do not need to *own* a horse to have a career with horses), support a car, build a kitty for medical expenses, or save to buy a farm of your own some day.

The best way to avoid burnout or disillusionment early in your career is to be brutally honest with yourself about the level of income you personally feel is comfortable. While you may not make that much money in your first job, your career choice should be able to provide it within a few years or you will not stay with the job. Do not just think about today and next month. Think about next year and the year after that. Look as far down the road as you can.

Deciding on your income goal may seem backward. You have to accept what employers offer, right? If you go into business for yourself, you can only charge what the market will bear for lessons, boarding, or hoof care, right? Certainly there is a "going rate" for various types of jobs and services. That rate will probably vary from one region of the country to another in response to the variable costs of living in one place or another.

However, psychologists tell us that setting goals is very important. Without a goal, you will simply settle for whatever is offered. If that level of income is not comfortable, you may tolerate it for awhile but eventually your economic discomfort will force you to leave the job. You (and possibly your employer) will end up with bad feelings that could have been avoided. If you had determined in advance that you needed a certain income to be comfortable (however you define that), you might have rejected the job in the first place. You would have been able to predict that the low wages would eventually make you feel unhappy and unappreciated. Indeed, you might have chosen another career altogether.

How to set your goal

Figuring your income comfort level is not a complicated accounting exercise. Rough estimates in round figures on an annual basis

WORKSHEET ON DESIRED INCOME

Put all estimates on the same basis—weekly, monthly, or annual

$ _____ . _____   Housing

_____   Utilities (heat, electricity, water, telephone)

_____   Food

_____   Clothing

_____   Health Insurance (if not provided by employer)

_____   Car or Truck Purchase (spread over the life of the loan)

_____   Gas, Oil, Repairs and Maintenance

_____   Car or Truck Insurance

_____   Horse Purchase (as one-time cost or spread over several years)

_____   Board

_____   Farrier Care

_____   Veterinary Care

_____   Tack and Other Equipment

_____   Trainer's Fees

_____   Show Expenses

_____   Entertainment

_____   Travel

_____   Savings

_____   Miscellaneous

$ _____ . _____   **Subtotal: Income needed before taxes**

_____   Taxes (employees add 25 percent; entrepreneurs add 32 percent)

$ _____ . _____   **TOTAL: Gross Income Desired**

will give you a good guide.

$$ Start by adding up the cost of basics such as housing, utilities, food, and clothing. At a minimum, add health insurance (which may be provided by some employers).

$$ What about transportation? How will you get to work? If you need a car or truck, add the cost of the car, gas, and insurance. If horse ownership is essential to your happiness, add bills for boarding, veterinary care, farrier care, plus trainers' fees and show expenses if you want to compete.

$$ How often do you plan to eat out, go to movies, rent a video, buy horse books, subscribe to horse magazines, or travel to visit friends and family? Give some thought to the things you can't live without and assign a ballpark figure. The income worksheet on page 32 is only a guideline. Add or remove living expenses to make it your own personal financial picture.

$$ Now add everything up. But wait! You are not through yet. The U.S. Internal Revenue Service takes a slice from everyone's paycheck or profits to support our national government. State governments may line up for their tax cut, too. The figure in front of you is the before-tax income you think you need to be comfortable. Whether you are working for someone else or running your own business, you need to add something to your net figure to pay for your federal, state, and local taxes. Assuming you are a single person with standard deductions, add about 25 percent of your net figure if you plan to work for someone else—or 32 percent if you think you will start your own business—as a rough estimate of your tax liability. Add that to the before-tax income figure to come up with a general idea of the **gross** annual income or salary you would like to have.

$$ Now divide your gross income figure by 12 or 52 to come up with the monthly or weekly income that is comfortable for you. When you evaluate a specific horse industry career, you now have a way to gauge whether the potential earnings are sufficient to put you in your economic comfort zone.

$$ You can now flip this exercise around and look at the prevailing wages for the horse industry jobs that appeal to you (see Chapter 7). Working backward, you can figure out what kind of lifestyle those wages would support, given your personal expenses. If there is an enormous gap between the income offered and the income you would like to have, you need to figure out how to close it. Maybe horse ownership can wait a few years. Perhaps someone would be interested in sharing a horse you already

own— and the expenses—for awhile. Public transportation or carpooling with co-workers might reduce the expense of getting to work. You may be willing to postpone wardrobe updates for awhile in order to have your dream career. Subsidies from relatives may help support the early stages of your career. Or maybe you need to broaden your career search to include other types of jobs in the horse industry.

You have just estimated the income you need to be comfortable today. Another important question is: What kind of income do you want to earn in ten years? It may seem hard to envision the future, but close your eyes and imagine yourself turning thirty or even forty. Will you still be living in the same type of housing? Will you have a family to support? Have you bought a horse or several horses? Are you driving the same car or truck? Does your job offer more responsibility now? Have you bought or leased the farm you need to establish your own base of operations?

Now comes an even more important question. What are you doing now? Will the job you are considering in the immediate future prepare you for what you want to be doing in ten years?

In the short run, you may feel that you can accept a lower than *comfortable* standard of living as a temporary situation because you see the job as a stepping stone to your long-range goal. The key words here are *stepping stone*. If the job is a dead-end position rather than the bottom rung on a true career ladder, it will not only prevent you from getting closer to your career goal, it will actually hold you back. In your eagerness to work with horses, do not fall into an economic trap. The time you spend in a dead-end job is time lost on the road to career success.

Have you ever heard the phrase *self-fulfilling prophecy*? It means that when we *think* something may happen, our subconscious directs us to choose actions that will *make* that something occur. Unconsciously, we fulfill our own prophecy. Athletes and others who mentally visualize success, who envision themselves winning, are harnessing the power of their subconscious to help them succeed.

The combination of conscious planning and harnessing your subconscious to keep you on track is a powerful one. By setting career goals now for your thirties or forties and even beyond, then visualizing the career ladder you must climb to achieve those goals, you actually prime your subconscious to help you succeed.

THE RICH LIFE

If you study the fifty careers outlined in Chapter 7, it will quickly become obvious that the horse industry is not a place where people make great fortunes. While an occasional trainer or manufacturer or event organizer may do well enough to attract a good bit of attention, few are becoming wealthy.

One reason is competition. So many people find the horse industry an attractive place to work that employers almost always enjoy a buyers' market. Anyone who starts an equine-related business that begins to turn decent profits will soon have dozens of imitators attempting to duplicate his success.

Another factor is the number of people working primarily in one area but moonlighting in another area to supplement their main income. The trainer who also sells articles to horse publications is one example. There are also many people eager to make some money—*any* money—from their horse hobby. Because they regard such income as "extra" money to pay for horse show fees or buy a specific item they want, they often fail to charge enough to provide a profit or income beyond covering their expenses. Their costs are often hidden among other everyday expenses, so they do not recognize and count them against their hobby earnings. This makes it harder for the person working full-time in the same profession to make a living wage. Another example is the neighbor who attends a weekend farrier school, then as a favor offers to do your horses for $20 less than your regular farrier.

If earnings potential is not a motivation to work in the horse industry, what is? People already in the industry have a hard time answering that question themselves. The beauty, intelligence, and power of horses captivated man's imagination long before the Greek Xenophon first wrote his classic treatise on training them. For many, the attraction to horses borders on an addiction for which there is no cure. Perhaps recognition of fellow addicts is the element that binds horse people together in a uniquely supportive community. Ask anyone who has been in the industry for twenty or thirty years if they wish they had made another choice, and inevitably they get around to telling you how fortunate they feel because they were able to make their passion a profession.

Planning your career path, rather than just waiting for a career to happen to you, is the best way to ensure not only that high level of job satisfaction but also a decent living.

CAREER CLOSE-UP

MANUFACTURER

Susan Domizi started her career in the horse industry as a working student sleeping in a hayloft because the house she was to live in wasn't finished yet. Still, she recalls crawling into her sleeping bag each night to sleep with the mice and the barn swallows and feeling privileged to be in the employ of a top horse professional, poised to set the show world on fire with her horsemanship prowess.

Though Susan's original dream was never fulfilled, a better one came true. Her talented event horse was plagued by shelly feet. When she discovered a seaweed-based product from Ireland that appeared to help him, she was ecstatic. However, the quality of the imported product was extremely inconsistent. Trained as a biochemist, Susan felt she could do better. So began an odyssey that resulted in the formation of a nutritional supplement company known as Source, Inc.

Domizi's intense research into the benefits of seaweed meals led to a product whose benefits for not only poor feet but also weight problems, coat condition, appetite, stress, and other nutritionally related conditions are now renowned among horsemen. Along the way she has developed harvesting and drying techniques that make the various seaweed meals used in Source among the highest quality in the world. She helped launch an organization dedicated to protecting precious coastal seaweed beds from pollution or over-harvesting and built a strong company able to prevail in the market against copycat competitors.

Susan attributes her success to an unwavering commitment to quality control, fair and equal treatment of all those she meets in the business world, and respect for her customers. From its very first pail, Domizi has sold Source with a money-back guarantee, the first of its kind in the horse industry. She points with pride to a shelf full of notebooks stuffed with letters from joyous horse owners whose horses improved when Source was added to their diets.

Susan's training as an analytical scientist gave her a model on which to build her business success. "Education in any field is useful because it teaches you how to learn and how to seek the answers you need," said Susan. Every step in the development and growth of her company has been supported by careful research, consultation with experts, and meticulous planning of all details. Source's longevity is legend in a market where many nutritional supplements blaze as a feeding fad for several years only to be discarded for lack of consistent results. Indeed, clamor among its customers has led to nutritional supplements for both humans and dogs based on the original Source formula.

Like many in the horse industry, Susan works long and hard to achieve success. In fact, managing her business now leaves no time for riding or a horse of her own. Still, Susan finds fulfillment in the stories about horses with nutritional problems whose lives were turned around by her product. She points with pride to the photo of a highly successful, famous racehorse whose dam was fed Source and who received Source from the time he was born. She smiles as she tells of horsemen who whisper in the shedrows about their "secret" for raising runners better able to withstand the rigors of racing than their peers. And it all started with her love of a big-hearted event horse named Hull. ■

Chapter 3

Educational Options

You have looked at your career choices, analyzed the skills necessary to prepare for the careers, and talked to people in those fields about the combination of education and experience you will need to qualify for a job.

Depending on the skills you plan to acquire through education to qualify for your chosen career, you have several options that vary in cost, time commitment, and academic depth:

🏛 trade schools offering certificates or diplomas for completing a training program in a specific skill

🏛 two-year colleges offering Associate in Arts (A.A.) or Associate in Applied Sciences (A.A.S.) degrees in equine studies

🏛 four-year colleges and universities offering Bachelor of Arts (B.A.) and Bachelor of Science (B.S.) degrees in equine studies, animal science, related agricultural sciences; or fields such as retailing, accounting, or communications that can be related to the horse industry

🏛 universities offering advanced degrees in agriculture or veterinary medicine including Doctor of Veterinary Medicine (D.V.M.), Master of Arts (M.A.), Master of Science (M.S.), and Doctor of Education (Ed.D.) or Philosophy (Ph.D.).

While a college degree is not an automatic guarantee of higher wages, it is generally true that more education translates into more income. Studies indicate that earning power goes up as much as 6 to 12 percent for every year of college education.

While a college education may not be essential in fields like stable management, riding instruction, retailing, or fence contracting, career experts still say the more years of college, the better. Many horse industry employers say they prefer employees with at least minimal college background because they feel these job candidates have better business sense, better interpersonal skills, and greater maturity. For client-centered operations such as horse show management or riding lesson programs, those skills and attitudes show up on the bottom line. They are just as essential, sometimes more so, than horse-related skills. Farriers, instructors, trainers, or anyone else considering going into business for themselves also need minimal bookkeeping and accounting skills, communications training, marketing background, and management skills if their businesses are to thrive. Formal education can provide them with the tools for success.

Another reason college-level education is prudent is that very few people stay in their first, or even second, job throughout their working years. Career specialists point out that the most common employment pattern of the future will be a series of jobs, even serial careers that may require picking up new skills periodically along the way. An education that is not purely horse specific can prepare you better for those future job shifts by providing a broad skill base.

Degrees in fields such as marketing, business, journalism, or engineering—where skills are not necessarily horse specific—can open the door to well-paying jobs in the horse industry while offering a lot of future flexibility. Many professionals in these fields earn part of their income from horse clients and part from clients in entirely different fields. An accountant might focus on clients who own Thoroughbred breeding farms *and* those with other agricultural businesses, such as beef cattle or hogs. A dual-

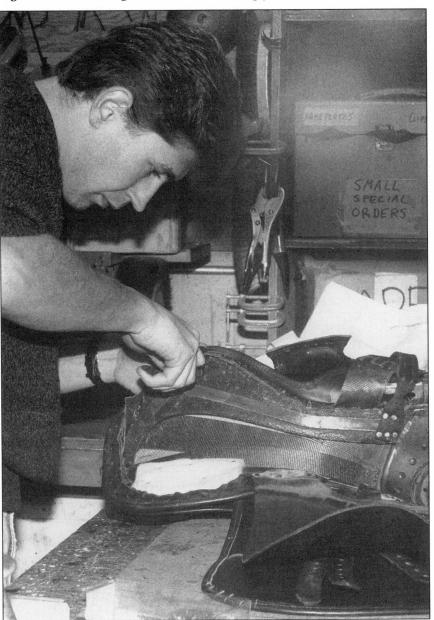

Saddle making is an intricate and highly skilled craft. There are many trade schools that offer specialty degrees in saddle-making.

HOW EDUCATION AFFECTS EARNINGS

Percent of workers by their usual weekly earnings and education level.
Reprinted from the U.S. Department of Commerce,
Occupational Outlook Quarterly / Winter 1994-1995

PERCENT OF
WORKERS

Less than a bachelor's degree
Bachelor's degree or higher

USUAL WEEKLY EARNINGS

purpose degree can boost your earning potential and give you more options should you want to change jobs or move to another geographic area.

If you do decide to focus your academic training narrowly on equine studies, evaluate any college-level program carefully in relationship to your long-term career goals. Most of these programs emphasize one phase of the horse industry over another, simply because of the limitation in the number of courses they can fit into each semester. If the program's emphasis is equitation, training, breeding, or general horse care, be sure that is your career goal. A program emphasizing general horse care might prepare you to work as a groom or tack shop sales staff. If you want to teach riding, however, look for a program that emphasizes equitation and teaching skills.

TRADE SCHOOLS AND SHORT COURSES

Trade school courses emphasize a single skill such as farriery, saddle making, or becoming a packer or guide; they can last anywhere from a few weeks to a year or more and those who finish them usually get a certificate of completion or a diploma. Short courses are intense programs in a particular skill such as broodmare management or farrier science; often only a week or two long, they are offered regularly by colleges and universities with equine or animal science degree programs. Depending on their course content, some of these programs will be appropriate for people preparing in depth for a specific career, while others will be more suited for people already working in the same or a related field who want additional skills or credentials.

For example, you might take a year-long beginning farrier's course with an eye to setting up your own shoeing business. A broodmare manager might take an eight-week course so he can trim his own mares to lower the farm's operating costs. Working farriers might attend an intense weekend workshop to learn new forging techniques. Make sure the course and the depth of instruction are really suitable for your career goals.

Choose a trade school carefully because the certificate or diploma you receive will be only as good as the school's reputation. Do not be dazzled by fancy brochures, and be wary of employment promises. Ask lots of questions:

☞ *Who runs the school? Who are the instructors? What are their reputations?* Does the school's operator have a solid reputation in the career field you aspire to? Ask around. If his or her reputation is not strong and positive among fellow horsemen, your certificate or diploma may actually become a liability instead of an asset when you apply for jobs. How strong are the instructor's credentials, both as a teacher and as a practitioner in the field? Those are separate skills. You may be attracted to a particular school because of endorsements by well-known horsemen in brochures that imply they will be teachers or clinicians. Find out in advance if their involvement is limited to that brochure blurb so you will not be disappointed.

☞ *How long has the school been operating?* A school with a short history is not necessarily one to avoid, just one to investigate more thoroughly. However, you don't want the school's money to run out before your training period is finished. Check with the local Better Business Bureau in the community where the school is located to see if there have been complaints about the school from former students. Call the information operator in the area where the school is located and ask for the Better Business Bureau's phone number or contact the Council of Better Business Bureaus (4200 Wilson Blvd., Arlington, VA 22203; 703-276-0100) and give them the zip code where the school is located to find out which local bureau to call. Ask who accredits the school.

☞ *What is the ratio of classroom theory to hands-on practice?* If you have come to learn how to shoe a horse or make a saddle, you shouldn't leave without putting your hands on a lot of leather or hooves. In many specialized fields like farriery, experience counts. The sooner you start getting it and the more you get, the better.

☞ *Will you leave the course ready to go to work?* Ask for the names of several graduates; then contact them to see if they felt their course preparation fully prepared them to go to work. Find out before you commit your tuition money if there will be additional skills you will need to acquire before you are fully qualified in the field. If the career you are preparing for calls for special tools, is a set of tools part of your tuition? Are they something you must purchase before or after your course? If the school provides tools, are they of sufficient quality to allow you to do quality course work?

☞ *Does the school provide any help with job leads or placement?* Most trade schools do not. However, if the school's recruitment literature promises to do so—or that "over 75 percent" or even

"100 percent" of their graduates find horse industry jobs—check out those claims carefully. What kinds of jobs did the graduates find? Did they find them on their own or with the school's help? Does the school maintain active contacts in the horse industry to generate job leads for its graduates? Did they find those jobs right after taking the course, six months later, or a year later? Were they good jobs at good pay? Did that extravagant claim apply only to a single class of four people who went through the program five years ago? Talking to *recent* graduates (or, better yet, their current employers) is one of the best ways of judging the validity of placement promises.

The following are some certificate programs offering instruction in specific skills (complete addresses are in the Appendix):

AUCTIONEERING

World Wide College of Auctioneering Inc., Mason City, IA 50402

FARRIERY

C.S. Mott Community College, Flint, MI 48503

Canadian School of Horseshoeing, Guelph, Ontario N1H 6H8, Canada

Casey and Son Horseshoeing School, Lafayette, GA 30728

Colby Community College, Colby, KS 67701

Colorado School of Trades, Lakewood, CO 80215

Colorado State University, Fort Collins, CO 80523

Cornell University, Ithaca, NY 14853

Dawson Community College, Glendive, MT 59330

Eastern School of Farriery, Martinsville, VA 24114

Far Hills Forge, Far Hills, NJ 07931

Florida School of Horseshoeing, Belleville, MI 48111

Gulf Coast Farriers School, Alvin, TX 77511

Kentucky Horseshoeing School, Mount Eden, KY 40046

Kwantlen College, Surrey, British Columbia V3T 5H8, Canada

Lamar Community College, Lamar, CO 81052

Linn–Benton Community College, Albany, OR 97321

Lookout Mountain School of Horseshoeing, Gadsden, AL 35901

Merced College, Merced, CA 95340

Meredith Manor International Equestrian Centre, Waverly, WV 26184

Mesa Technical College, Tucumcari, NM 88401

Michigan School of Horseshoeing, Belleville, MI 48111

Midwest Horseshoeing School, Macomb, IL 61455

Minnesota School of Horseshoeing, Ramsey, MN 55303
Montana State University, Bozeman, MT 59717
North Texas Farrier's School, Mineral Wells, TX 76068
Northwest College, Powell, WY 82435-1898
Northwest Missouri State University, Maryville, MO 64468
Oklahoma Farrier's College, Inc., Sperry, OK 74073
Oklahoma Horseshoeing School, Oklahoma City, OK 73111
Oklahoma State Horseshoeing School, Ardmore, OK 73401
Olds College, Olds, Alberta T0M 1P0, Canada
Otterbein College, Westerville, OH 43081
Pacific Coast Horseshoeing School, Sacramento, CA 95829
Pike's Peak Community College, Colorado Springs, CO 80920
Saint Mary-of-the-Woods College, Saint Mary-of-the-Woods,
   IN 47846-1099
Seneca College of Applied Arts & Technology, King City, Ontario
   L0G 1K0, Canada
Shur Shod Shoeing School, Cimarron, KS 67835
Sierra Equestrian, Bishop, CA 93514
South Puget Sound Community College, Olympia, WA 98502
Sul Ross State University, Alpine, TX 79832
Tennesee State Blacksmith & Farrier School, Bloomington
   Springs, TN 38545
Texas Horseshoeing School, Scurry, TX 75158
Texas State Horseshoeing School, Weatherford, TX 76086
Tucson School of Horseshoeing, Tucson, AZ 85749
Tucumcari Farrier Technologies, Tucumcari, NM 88401
University of Wisconsin–River Falls, River Falls, WI 54022
Walla Walla Community College, WallaWalla, WA 99362
Western Nevada Community College, Carson City, NV 89703
Western's School of Horseshoeing, Phoenix, AZ 85017
Wolverine Farrier School, Howell, MI 48843

HANDICAPPED-RIDING INSTRUCTION

Cheff Center for the Handicapped, Augusta, MI 49012
Lakeshore Technical College, Cleveland, WI 53015

HORSE TRAINING

Brookdale Community College, Lincroft, NJ 07738
Meredith Manor International Equestrian Centre, Waverly,
   WV 26184
North Central Texas College, Gainesville, TX 76240
Scottsdale Community College, Scottsdale, AZ 85250

MASSAGE THERAPY

Equine Sports Massage Program, Ocala, FL 34473
Equissage, Southern Pines, NC 28388
EquiTouch Systems, Antelope, CA 95843

RACING

Hawkeye Hill Racing School, Commiskey, IN 47227
Rancho Del Castillo, Winter Haven, FL 33880
White Wood Farm, Killingworth, CT 06419

RIDING INSTRUCTION

Black Hawk College, Kewanee, IL 61443
Kemptville College of Agricultural Technology, Kemptville,
    Ontario K0G1J0, Canada
Meredith Manor International Equestrian Centre, Waverly,
    WV 26184
Ogonz Equestrian Center, Lisbon, NH 03585
Rawhide Vocational College, Bonsall, CA 92003
Scottsdale Community College, Scottsdale, AZ 85250
Woodcock Hill Riding Academy, Willington, CT 06279

SADDLE MAKING

Oklahoma State Univ.-Technical Branch, Okmulgee, OK 74447
Sierra Equestrian, Bishop, CA 93514

STABLE OR FARM MANAGEMENT

Black Hawk College, Kewanee, IL 61443
Brookdale Community College, Lincroft, NJ 07738
Central Florida Community College, Hackettstown, NJ 07840
College of Southern Idaho, Twin Falls, ID 83301
College of the Redwoods, Eureka, CA 95501
Kemptville College of Agricultural Technology, Kemptville,
    Ontario K0G1J0, Canada
Kentucky Horse Park Education Dept., Lexington, KY 40511
King's River Community College, Reedley, CA 93654
Kirkwood Community College, Cedar Rapids, IA 52406
Los Angeles Pierce College, Woodland Hills, CA 91371
Meredith Manor International Equestrian Centre, Waverly,
    WV 26184
Michigan State University, East Lansing, MI 48824-1225
Mt. San Antonio College, Walnut, CA 91789
North Central Texas College, Gainesville, TX 76240

Ogonz Equestrian Center, Lisbon, NH 03585
Parkland College, Champaign, IL 61821
Rawhide Vocational College, Bonsall, CA 92003
Rogers State College, Claremore, OK 74017
Sierra College, Rocklin, CA 95677-3397
State University of New York–Cobleskill, Cobleskill, NY 12043
White Wood Farm, Killingworth, CT 06419

WRANGLER GUIDE

Feather River College, Quincy, CA 95971
Rush's Lakeview Outfitter and Guide School, Lima, MT 59739

TWO-YEAR DEGREE PROGRAMS

Two-year degree programs concentrate on equine studies, veterinary technology, or animal science. It is important to be sure that the program's focus is a good fit with your career choice.

Some equine studies programs focus narrowly on a particular skill or set of skills such as farriery, riding instruction, ranch management, or breeding farm management almost in the same way a trade school does. These programs are best suited for people who are certain they will not attend more than two years of college and have a definite career in mind when they enroll.

If you are not positive about your career goals, an equine program that gives students a broader background in business, communication, or general sciences along with basic equine courses on health, feeding, and handling leaves your career commitment a little more open ended. These courses are better suited for the person who thinks they might transfer to a four-year program. Some two-year programs are also designed to prepare students who intend to apply to veterinary schools.

The American Veterinary Medical Association accredits two-year (and four-year) veterinary-technology degree programs that qualify graduates to assist veterinarians. Many states now license veterinary technicians, and a degree from one of these college-level programs is sometimes a requirement for certification. Veterinary technology programs are not specifically equine courses. Graduates are qualified to work with either large- or small-animal veterinarians, which broadens their future job options.

A U.S. Department of Commerce survey of high-paying occupations identified health technology as an area where those with less than a four-year degree could look forward to weekly earnings of $700 or more. Other good paying opportunities for non-degree holders that could be given an equestrian spin included the areas of carpentry, mechanical engineering, insurance sales and adjusting, marketing, advertising, public relations, purchasing, and real estate; and such jobs as sales representatives, science technicians, secretaries, truck drivers, and computer operators.

The education vs. experience debate that we pointed out in Chapter 2 probably applies to two-year equine studies programs more than to any of the other education options. If you have little or no experience with horses prior to enrolling, do not expect that employers will consider you fully qualified to take responsibility for their horses once you hold a two-year equine studies degree. That is particularly true for the more general programs.

Horse industry employers hiring people for jobs working directly with horses are quite blunt that they will almost always take the person with solid horse experience over the job candidate holding a piece of paper from an equine studies program. At the same time, the degree holder with experience holds a decided edge over the experienced job candidate with no education beyond high school. Their additional business and people skills tip the scales in their favor, just as they can look forward to higher lifetime earnings.

Many of the caveats discussed for trade schools also apply to two-year schools. Who are the instructors? What are their credentials? Who accredits the school? What is the ratio of classroom theory to hands-on experience? Again, look carefully at claims of high placement rates. Recent graduates should be able to verify them and there should be evidence of an active placement effort to find jobs that offer decent wages.

In a 1991 study by equine educator Dr. Sue Stuska, 20 two-year colleges reported that an average of 82 percent of their equine studies graduates were employed in the horse industry. The educators estimated that from 8 to 50 percent of their graduates would go on to earn a four-year degree while up to 30 percent were unemployed. Of the graduates employed in the horse industry, 25 percent worked as stable/farm workers or managers; 21 percent were teaching riding, training horses, or involved in equestrian recreation; 18 percent worked in the horse show industry as grooms or show personnel; 10 percent entered the racing industry, primarily as grooms; and 2 percent worked in communications or the arts.

SCHOOLS WITH TWO-YEAR EQUINE DEGREES OR RELATED OFFERINGS

Allen County Community College, Iola, KS 66749
Berry College, Mount Berry, GA 30149-0326
Black Hawk College, Kewanee, IL 61443
Blue Ridge Community College, Weyers Cave, VA 24486
Brigham Young University, Provo, UT 84602
Cazenovia College, Cazenovia, NY 13035
Cecil Community College, North East MD 21901
Central Texas College, Killeen, TX 76540
Central Wyoming College, Riverton, WY 82501
Colby Community College, Colby, KS 67701
Colby–Sawyer College, New London, NH 03257
College of Southern Idaho, Twin Falls, ID 83301
Connors State College, Warner, OK 74469
Dawson Community College, Glendive, MT 59330
Dodge City Community College, Dodge City, KS 67801
Eastern Wyoming College, Torrington, WY 82240
Feather River College, Quincy, CA 95971
Green River Community College, Auburn, WA 98002
Hiwassee College, Madisonville, TN 37354
Illinois Valley Community College, Oglesby, IL 61348-1099
Johnson County Community College, Overland Park, KS 66210
Lakeshore Technical College, Cleveland, WI 53015
Lamar Community College, Lamar, CO 81052
Laramie County Community College, Cheyenne, WY 82007
Lassen College, Susanville, CA 96130
Lord Fairfax Community College, Middletown, VA 22645
Los Angeles Pierce College, Woodland Hills, CA 91371
Martin Community College, Williamston, NC 27892
Mesa Technical College, Tucumcari, NM 88401
Morehead State University, Morehead, KY 40351
Mount Ida College, Newton Center, MA 02159
Northeastern Junior College, Sterling, CO 80751-2399
Northwest College, Powell, WY 82435-1898
Northwestern State Univeristy of Louisiana, Natchitoches,
    LA 71497
Ohio State University, Wooster, OH 44691
Pace University, Pleasantville, NY 10570-2799
Parkland College, Champaign, IL 61821
Purdue University, West Lafayette, IN 47907-7677
Redlands Community College, El Reno, OK 73036

Rogers State College, Claremore, OK 74017

Saint Mary-of-the-Woods College, Saint Mary-of-the-Woods,
   IN 47846-1099

Salem–Teikyo University, Salem, WV 26426

Scottsdale Community College, Scottsdale, AZ 85250

Shasta College, Redding, CA 96049

Sheridan College, Sheridan, WY 82801

Sierra College, Rocklin, CA 95677-3397

Southern Virgnia College for Women, Buena Vista, VA 24416

State University of New York–Cobleskill, Cobleskill, NY 12043

State University of New York–Delhi, Delhi, NY 13753

State University of New York–Morrisville, Morrisville, NY 13408

Stephens College, Columbia, MO 65215

Sul Ross State University, Alpine, TX 79832

Teikyo Post University, Waterbury, CT 06723-2540

University of Connecticut, Storrs, CT 06269-4040

University of Findlay, Findlay, OH 45840

University of Georgia, Athens, GA 30602

University of Maine–Orono, Orono, ME 04469

Virginia Highlands Community College, Abingdon, VA 24212

Western Wyoming Community College, Rock Springs, WY 82902

Wilson College, Chambersburg, PA 17201

Wood Junior College, Mathiston, MS 39752

SCHOOLS WITH TWO-YEAR VETERINARY TECHNOLOGY DEGREES

Becker College, Leicester, MA 01524

Berry College, Mount Berry, GA 30149-0326

Blue Ridge Community College, Weyers Cave, VA 24486

Brigham Young, University Provo, UT 84602

Camden County College, Blackwood, NJ 08012

Cedar Valley College, Lancaster, TX 75134

Central Carolina Community College, Sanford, NC 27330

Colby Community College, Colby, KS 67701

Colorado Mountain College, Glenwood Springs, CO 81601

Columbia State Community College, Columbia, TN 38401

Columbus State Community College, Columbus, OH 43216

Consumnes River College, Sacramento, CA 95823

Eastern Wyoming College, Torrington, WY 82240

Essex Community College, Baltimore, MD 21237

Fairmont State College, Fairmont, WV 26554

Foothill College, Los Altos Hills, CA 94022

Fort Valley State College, Fort Valley, GA 31030

Harcum Junior College, Bryn Mawr, PA 19010

Hartnell College, Salina, CA 939001

Hinds Community College, Raymond, MS 39154

Holyoke Community College, Holyoke, MA 01040-1099

Jefferson College, Hillsboro, MO 63050

Kirkwood Community College, Cedar Rapids, IA 52406

La Guardia Community College, Long Island City, NY 11101

Lincoln Memorial University, Harrogate, TN 37752

Los Angeles Pierce College, Woodland Hills, CA 91371

Macomb Community College, Mt. Clemens, MI 48044

Madison Area Technical College, Madison, WI 53704

Manor Junior College, Jenkintown, PA 19046

Maple Woods Community College, Kansas City, MO 64156

Medical Institute of Minnesota, Bloomington, MN 55437

Midland College, Midland, TX 79705

Morehead State University, Morehead, KY 40351

Mount Ida College, Newton Center, MA 02159

Mt. San Antonio College, Walnut, CA 91789

National College, Rapid City, SD 57709

Nebraska College of Technical Agriculture, Curtis, NE 69025

North Dakota State University, Fargo, ND 58105

Northern Virginia Community College, Sterling, VA 22170

Northwestern State Univeristy of Louisiana, Natchitoches,
     LA 71497

Omaha College of Health Careers, Omaha, NE 68154

Parkland College, Champaign, IL 61821

Pierce College at Fort Steilacoom, Tacoma, WA 98498

Portland Community College, Portland, OR 97219

Purdue University, West Lafayette, IN 47907-7677

Raymond Walters College, Cincinnati, OH 45221

San Diego Mesa College, San Diego, CA 92111

Snead State Community College, Boaz, AL 35957

St. Petersburg Junior College, St. Petersburg, FL 33733

State University of New York–Canton, Canton, NY 13617

State University of New York–Delhi, Delhi, NY 13753

State University of New York–Farmingdale, Farmingdale, NY 11735

Sul Ross State University, Alpine, TX 79832

Tomball College, Tomball, TX 77375-4036

Tri-County Technical College, Pendleton, SC 29670

University of Georgia, Athens, GA 30602

University of Maine–Orono, Orono, ME 04469

Vermont Technical College, Randolph Center, VT 05061

Wayne County Community College, Detroit, MI 48201
Willmar Technical College, Willmar, MN 56201
Wilson College, Chambersburg, PA 17201
Yuba College, Marysville, CA 95901

FOUR-YEAR PROGRAMS

The widest range of job opportunities are open to those holding four-year degrees. Like two-year colleges, there are four-year programs leading to a degree in equine science. Some focus on a particular sequence such as equitation and teaching while others put heavier emphasis on horse management and breeding.

A far greater number of degree programs are available in animal science and other agricultural fields such as agribusiness, agricultural engineering, agricultural economics, and agricultural communications. You may be able to combine one of these degree programs with an equine minor.

If you are not sure where to start looking for these programs, begin at your state's land-grant university. The Morrill Act of 1862 granted lands to states for the purpose of establishing schools for agricultural research and teaching. A second Morrill Act in 1890 added additional schools to this land-grant network. With a long tradition of teaching in the agricultural sciences, these land-grant universities have become respected research institutions with outstanding faculty. While not all of them offer programs specifically geared to the equine industry, they can prepare you for many agricultural careers that mesh with the horse industry. There is at least one land-grant university in every state. Since most of them are also public institutions, the land-grant university in your state may also be your best tuition bargain.

Four-year degrees in fields like marketing, advertising, recreation, environmental sciences, accounting, biochemistry, animal biology, or natural resource management can also prepare you for jobs in the horse industry. Talk to admissions personnel to discuss your career goals and see whether a minor in equine studies or animal science can be combined with your chosen major.

FOUR-YEAR SCHOOLS WITH EQUINE OR ANIMAL SCIENCE DEGREES

Alfred University, Angelica, NY 14709
Auburn University, Auburn, AL 36849-5528
Averett College, Danville, VA 24541

Berry College Mount, Berry, GA 30149-0326
Black Forest Hall, Harbor Springs, MI 49740
Brigham Young University, Provo, UT 84602
California Polytechnic State University, Pomona, CA 91768
California State University–Fresno, Fresno, CA 93740-0075
Cazenovia College, Cazenovia, NY 13035
Centenary College, Hackettstown, NJ 07840
Clemson University, Clemson, SC 29634
Colorado State University, Fort Collins, CO 80523
Delaware Valley College of Science and Agriculture, Doylestown,
    PA 18901
Elms College, Chicopee, MA 01013
Ferrum College, Ferrum, VA 24088
Iowa State University, Ames, IA 50011
Johnson & Wales University, Providence, RI 02903
Judson College, Marion, AL 36756
Kansas State University, Manhattan, KS 66506
Lake Erie College, Painesville, OH 44077
Louisiana State University, Baton Rouge, LA 70803
Louisiana Tech University, Ruston, LA 71272
Michigan State University, East Lansing, MI 48824-1225
Middle Tennessee State University, Murfreesboro, TN 37132
Midway College, Midway, KY 40347-1120
Mississippi State University, Mississippi State, MS 39762
Morehead State University, Morehead, KY 40351
Mount Ida College, Newton Center, MA 02159
Mount Senario College, Ladysmith, WI 54848
Murray State University, Murray, KY 42071
New Mexico State University, Las Cruces, NM 30003
North Carolina State University, Raleigh, NC 27695-7621
Northeast Louisiana University, Monroe, LA 71209-0510
Northeast Missouri State University, Kirksville, MO 63501
Northwest Missouri State University, Maryville, MO 64468
Northwestern State Univeristy of Louisiana, Natchitoches,
    LA 71497
Ohio State University, Columbus, OH 43210
Oklahoma State University, Stillwater, OK 74078-0102
Oregon State University, Corvallis, OR 97331-6702
Otterbein College, Westerville, OH 43081
Pace University, Pleasantville, NY 10570-2799
Pennsylvania State University, University Park, PA 16802
Purdue University, West Lafayette, IN 47907-7677

Rocky Mountain College, Billings, MT 59102

Rutgers University, New Brunswick, NJ 08903-0231

Saint Mary-of-the-Woods College, Saint Mary-of-the-Woods,
    IN 47846-1099

Salem–Teikyo University, Salem, WV 26426

South Dakota State University, Brookings, SD 57007

Southern Illinois University–Carbondale, Carbondale, IL 62901

Southwest Missouri State University, Springfield, MO 65802

St. Andrews Presbyterian College, Laurinburg, NC 28352

State University of New York–Cobleskill, Cobleskill, NY 12043

Stephens College, Columbia, MO 65215

Sul Ross State University, Alpine, TX 79832

Tarlton State University, Stephensville, TX 76402

Teikyo Post University, Waterbury, CT 06723-2540

Texas A&M University, College Station, TX 77843

Texas Tech University, Lubbock, TX 79409

University of Arizona, Tuscon, AZ 85721

University of California–Davis, Davis, CA 95616

University of Connecticut, Storrs, CT 06269-4040

University of Delaware, Newark, DE 19717-1303

University of Findlay, Findlay, OH 45840

University of Florida, Gainesville, FL 32611

University of Georgia, Athens, GA 30602

University of Idaho, Moscow, ID 83843

University of Illinois, Champaign-Urbana, IL 61801

University of Kentucky, Lexington, KY 40506

University of Louisville, Louisville, KY 40292

University of Maine–Orono, Orono, ME 04469

University of Maryland, College Park, MD 20742

University of Massachusetts, Amherst, MA 01003

University of Minnesota–Crookston, Crookston, MN 56716

University of Missouri–Columbia, Columbia, MO 65211

University of Nevada, Reno, NV 89557-0104

University of New Hampshire, Durham, NH 03824

University of Rhode Island, Kingston, RI 02881-0804

University of Tennessee, Knoxville, TN 37996

University of Vermont, Burlington, VT 05405

University of Wisconsin–River Falls, River Falls, WI 54022

Utah State University, Logan, UT 84322-4900

Virginia Intermont College, Bristol, VA 24201

Virginia Polytechnic Institute & State University, Blacksburg,
    VA 24061-0306

Washington State University, Pullman, WA 99164-6310
West Texas State University, Canyon, TX 79016
Western Kentucky University, Bowling Green, KY 42101
William Woods College, Fulton, MO 65251
Wilson College, Chambersburg, PA 17201

FOUR-YEAR SCHOOLS OFFERING PRE-VET DEGREES

Auburn University, Auburn, AL 36849-5528
Berry College, Mount Berry, GA 30149-0326
Brigham Young University, Provo, UT 84602
California Polytechnic State University, Pomona, CA 91768
California State University–Fresno, Fresno, CA 93740-0075
Clemson University, Clemson, SC 29634
Colorado State University, Fort Collins, CO 80523
Cornell University, Ithaca, NY 14853
Delaware Valley College of Science and Agriculture, Doylestown,
    PA 18901
Fairmont State College, Fairmont, WV 26554
Iowa State University, Ames, IA 50011
Kansas State University, Manhattan, KS 66506
Lake Erie College, Painesville, OH 44077
Louisiana State University, Baton Rouge, LA 70803
Louisiana Tech University, Ruston, LA 71272
Michigan State University, East Lansing, MI 48824-1225
Middle Tennessee State, University Murfreesboro, TN 37132
Mississippi State University, Mississippi State, MS 39762
Montana State University, Bozeman, MT 59717
Morehead State University, Morehead, KY 40351
Mount Ida College, Newton Center, MA 02159
Murray State University, Murray, KY 42071
New Mexico State University, Las Cruces, NM 30003
North Carolina State University, Raleigh, NC 27695-7621
North Dakota State University, Fargo , ND 58105
Northeast Louisiana University, Monroe, LA 71209-0510
Northeast Missouri State University, Kirksville, MO 63501
Northwestern State Univeristy of Louisiana, Natchitoches,
    LA 71497
Ohio State University, Columbus, OH 43210
Oklahoma State University, Stillwater, OK 74078-0102
Oregon State University, Corvallis, OR 97331-6702
Otterbein College, Westerville, OH 43081
Pace University, Pleasantville, NY 10570-2799

Pennsylvania State University, University Park, PA 16802
Purdue University, West Lafayette, IN 47907-7677
Quinnipiac College, Hamden, CT 06518
Rutgers University, New Brunswick, NJ 08903-0231
South Dakota State University, Brookings, SD 57007
Southern Illinois University–Carbondale, Carbondale, IL 62901
Southwest Missouri State University, Springfield, MO 65802
St. Andrews Presbyterian College, Laurinburg, NC 28352
State University of New York–Cobleskill, Cobleskill, NY 12043
Stephens College, Columbia, MO 65215
Sul Ross State University, Alpine, TX 79832
Tarlton State University, Stephensville, TX 76402
Teikyo Post University, Waterbury, CT 06723-2540
Texas A&M University, College Station, TX 77843
Texas Tech University, Lubbock, TX 79409
Tufts University, North Grafton, MA 01536
Tuskegee University, Tuskegee, AL 36088
University of Arizona, Tuscon, AZ 85721
University of California–Davis, Davis, CA 95616
University of Connecticut, Storrs, CT 06269-4040
University of Delaware, Newark, DE 19717-1303
University of Findlay, Findlay, OH 45840
University of Florida, Gainesville, FL 32611
University of Georgia, Athens, GA 30602
University of Guelph, Guelph, Ontario N1G 1W1, Canada
University of Illinois, Champaign–Urbana, IL 61801
University of Kentucky, Lexington, KY 40506
University of Louisville, Louisville, KY 40292
University of Maine–Orono, Orono, ME 04469
University of Maryland, College Park, MD 20742
University of Massachusetts, Amherst, MA 01003
University of Missouri–Columbia, Columbia, MO 65211
University of Nevada, Reno, NV 89557-0104
University of New Hampshire, Durham, NH 03824
University of Rhode Island, Kingston, RI 02881-0804
University of Rhode Island, Kingston, RI 02881
University of Tennessee, Knoxville, TN 37996
University of Vermont, Burlington, VT 05405
University of Wisconsin–River Falls, River Falls, WI 54022
Utah State University, Logan, UT 84322-4900
Virginia Polytechnic Institute & State University, Blacksburg,
    VA 24061-0306

Washington State University, Pullman, WA 99164-6310
West Texas State University, Canyon, TX 79016
Wilson College, Chambersburg, PA 17201

SCHOOLS OFFERING FOUR-YEAR VETERINARY TECHNOLOGY DEGREES

Fairmont State College, Fairmont, WV 26554
Mercy College, Dobbs Ferry, NY 10522
North Dakota State University, Fargo, ND 58105
Quinnipiac College, Hamden, CT 06518

LAND GRANT UNIVERSITIES

Alabama A&M University, Normal, AL 35762
Alcorn State University, Lorman, MS 39096
Auburn University, Auburn, AL 36849
Clemson University, Clemson, SC 29634
Colorado State University, Fort Collins, CO 80523
Cornell University, Ithaca, NY 14853
Delaware State College, Dover, DE 19901
Florida A&M University, Tallahassee, FL 32307
Iowa State University, Ames, IA 50011
Kansas State University, Manhattan, KS 66506
Kentucky State University, Frankfort, KY 40601
Langston University, Langston, OK 73050
Lincoln University, Jefferson City, MO 65101
Louisiana State University, Baton Rouge, LA 70803
Michigan State University, East Lansing, MI 48824-1225
Mississippi State University, Mississippi State, MS 39762
Montana State University, Bozeman, MT 59717
New Mexico State University, Las Cruces, NM 30003
North Carolina A&T State University, Greensboro, NC 27420
North Carolina State University, Raleigh, NC 27695-7621
North Dakota State University, Fargo, ND 58105
Ohio State University, Columbus, OH 43210
Oklahoma State University, Stillwater, OK 74078-0102
Oregon State University, Corvallis, OR 97331-6702
Pennsylvania State University, University Park, PA 16802
Prairie View A&M University, Prairie View, TX 77446-2867
Purdue University, West Lafayette, IN 47907-7677
Rutgers University, New Brunswick, NJ 08903-0231
South Carolina State College, Orangeburg, SC 29117
South Dakota State University, Brookings, SD 57007

Southern University and A&M College, Baton Rouge, LA 70813
Tennessee State University, Nashville, TN 37209-1561
Texas A&M University, College Station, TX 77843
The Fort Valley State College, Fort Valley, GA 31030
Tuskegee University, Tuskegee, AL 36088
University of Alaska, Fairbanks, AK 99775-5200
University of Arizona, Tuscon, AZ 85721
University of Arkansas, Little Rock, AR 72203
University of Arkansas, Pine Bluff, AR 71601
University of California–Oakland, Oakland, CA 94612-3560
University of Connecticut, Storrs, CT 06269-4040
University of Delaware, Newark, DE 19717-1303
University of Georgia, Athens, GA 30602
University of Hawaii, Honolulu, HI 96822
University of Idaho, Moscow, ID 83843
University of Kentucky, Lexington, KY 40506
University of Maine–Orono, Orono, ME 04469
University of Maryland, College Park, MD 20742
University of Maryland, Eastern Shore, MD 21853
University of Massachusetts, Amherst, MA 01003
University of Minnesota, St. Paul, MN 55108
University of Missouri–Columbia, Columbia, MO 65211
University of Nebraska, Lincoln, NE 68583-0703
University of Nevada, Reno, NV 89557-0104
University of New Hampshire, Durham, NH 03824
University of Rhode Island, Kingston, RI 02881-0804
University of Tennessee, Knoxville, TN 37996
University of the District of Columbia, Washington, DC 20008
University of Vermont, Burlington, VT 05405
University of Wyoming, Laramie, WY 82071
University of Wisconsin–Madison, Madison, WI 53706
Utah State University, Logan, UT 84322-4900
Virginia Polytechnic Institute & State University, Blacksburg,
    VA 24061-0306
Virginia State University, Petersburg, VA 23803
Washington State University, Pullman, WA 99164-6310
West Virginia University, Morgantown, WV 26506

ADVANCED DEGREES

A degree in veterinary medicine is the most well-known advanced degree for those interested in horse careers. However, advanced degrees in other fields, such as animal science, horse nutrition, agriculture, agricultural engineering, and agribusiness, can prepare you for fulfilling careers in many parts of the horse industry. Equipment manufacturers, feed companies, and associations need highly skilled job candidates who are prepared to help their businesses grow and prosper in the twenty-first century. Even degrees in nonhorse areas such as architecture, law, and accounting can be used to find a career niche in the horse industry.

The job profiles in Chapter 7 describe the type and amount of education you will need to meet specific career goals.

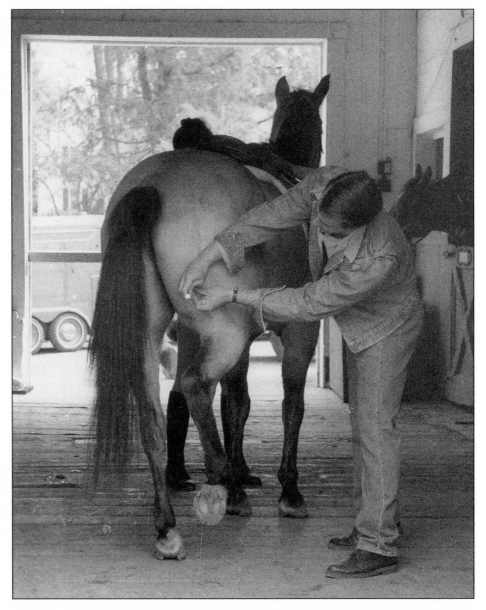

A veterinarian must obtain a graduate degree and pass government board exams.

SCHOOLS OFFERING ADVANCED EQUINE OR ANIMAL SCIENCE DEGREES

Auburn University, Auburn, AL 36849-5528
California Polytechnic State University, Pomona, CA 91768
California State University–Fresno, Fresno, CA 93740-0075
Clemson University, Clemson, SC 29634
Colorado State University, Fort Collins, CO 80523
Iowa State University, Ames, IA 50011
Kansas State University, Manhattan, KS 66506
Louisiana State University, Baton Rouge, LA 70803
Louisiana Tech University, Ruston, LA 71272
Michigan State University, East Lansing, MI 48824-1225
Morehead State University, Morehead, KY 40351
Murray State University, Murray, KY 42071
New Mexico State University, Las Cruces, NM 30003
North Carolina State University, Raleigh, NC 27695-7621
Ohio State University, Columbus, OH 43210
Oklahoma State University, Stillwater, OK 74078-0102
Oregon State University, Corvallis, OR 97331-6702
Pennsylvania State University, University Park, PA 16802
Purdue University, West Lafayette, IN 47907-7677
Rutgers University, New Brunswick, NJ 08903-0231
Salem-Teikyo University, Salem, WV 26426
Southern Illinois University–Carbondale, Carbondale, IL 62901
Southwest Missouri State University, Springfield, MO 65802
Tarlton State University, Stephensville, TX 76402
Texas A&M University, College Station, TX 77843
Texas Tech University, Lubbock, TX 79409
University of Arizona, Tuscon, AZ 85721
University of California–Davis, Davis, CA 95616
University of Connecticut, Storrs, CT 06269-4040
University of Delaware, Newark, DE 19717-1303
University of Florida, Gainesville, FL 32611
University of Georgia, Athens, GA 30602
University of Illinois, Champaign-Urbana, IL 61801
University of Maine–Orono, Orono, ME 04469
University of Maryland, College Park, MD 20742
University of Massachusetts, Amherst, MA 01003
University of Missouri–Columbia, Columbia, MO 65211
University of Nevada, Reno, NV 89557-0104
University of New Hampshire, Durham, NH 03824
University of Rhode Island, Kingston, RI 02881

University of Vermont, Burlington, VT 05405
Utah State University, Logan, UT 84322-4900
Virginia Polytechnic Institute & State University, Blacksburg, VA
24061-0306
Washington State University, Pullman, WA 99164-6310
West Texas State University, Canyon, TX 79016
William Woods College, Fulton, MO 65251

SCHOOLS OFFERING VETERINARY DEGREES

Auburn University, Auburn, AL 36849-5528
Colorado State University, Fort Collins, CO 80523
Cornell University, Ithaca, NY 14853
Iowa State University, Ames, IA 50011
Kansas State University, Manhattan, KS 66506
Louisiana State University, Baton Rouge, LA 70803
Michigan State University, East Lansing, MI 48824-1225
Mississippi State University, Mississippi State, MS 39762
North Carolina State University, Raleigh, NC 27695-7621
Ohio State University, Columbus, OH 43210
Oklahoma State University, Stillwater, OK 74078-0102
Oregon State University, Corvallis, OR 97331-6702
Purdue University, West Lafayette, IN 47907-7677
Texas A&M University, College Station, TX 77843
Tufts University, North Grafton, MA 01536
Tuskegee University, Tuskegee, AL 36088
University of California–Davis, Davis, CA 95616
University of Florida, Gainesville, FL 32611
University of Georgia, Athens, GA 30602
University of Guelph, Guelph, Ontario N1G 1W1, Canada
University of Illinois, Champaign-Urbana, IL 61801
University of Minnesota, St. Paul, MN 55108
University of Missouri–Columbia, Columbia, MO 65211
University of Pennsylvania, Philadelphia, PA 19104
University of Saskatchewan, Saskatoon, Saskatchewan S7N 0W0,
Canada
University of Tennessee, Knoxville, TN 37996
University of Wisconsin–Madison, Madison, WI 53706
Virginia-Maryland Regional College of Veterinary Medicine,
Blacksburg, VA 24061-0442
Washington State University, Pullman, WA 99164-6310

IF YOU HAVE TO RIDE

Enrolling in an equine degree program or studying animal science is not the only way to "horse around" on campus. Many schools have riding clubs that are open to anyone on campus, some have clubs for students enrolled in any of the animal sciences, and some even have rodeo clubs.

The **United States Polo Association** (4059 Iron Works Pike, Lexington, KY 40511; 606-255-0593) maintains a roster of schools that field intercollegiate polo teams. While some are on campuses offering equine or animal science programs, others are at decidedly non-aggie schools such as Harvard and Yale. You can earn your degree in accounting or business administration and play polo to bide your time until you head out into the world to find your niche in an agricultural business or association.

SCHOOLS WITH POLO PROGRAMS

*Polo clubs marked with an asterisk * are located at secondary schools.*

California Polytechnic Institute Polo Club, San Luis Obispo, CA 93407

Colorado State University Polo Club, Fort Collins, CO 80523

Cornell Polo Club, Ithaca, NY 14851

*Culver Military Academy Polo Club, Culver, IN 46511

*Garrison Forest School Polo Club, Owings Mills, MD 21117

Georgetown Polo Club, Sterling, VA 22170 (for students at Georgetown University)

Harvard University Polo Club, Cambridge, MA 02136

*Kent School Polo Club, Kent, CT 06757

Moorpark College Polo Association, Moorpark, CA 93021

Purdue Intercollegiate Polo Club, West Lafayette, IN 47907

Skidmore College Polo Club, West Charlton, NY 12010

Stanford University Polo Club, Portola Valley, CA 94028

Texas A&M University Polo Club, College Station, TX 77843

Texas Tech Polo Club, Lubbock, TX 79409

Tulane University Polo Club, New Orleans, LA 70118

University of California–Davis Polo Club, Davis, CA 95616

University of Connecticut Polo Club, Storrs, CT 06269

University of Oklahoma Polo Club, Norman, OK 73019

University of Santa Barbara Polo Club, Santa Barbara, CA 93106

University of Southern California Polo Club, Los Angeles, CA 90089-0273

University of Virginia Polo Club, Charlottesville, VA 22903

*Valley Forge Military Academy Polo Club, Wayne, PA 19087
Washington State University Polo Club, Pullman, WA 99163
Yale Polo Club, New Haven, CT 06020-8216

For over 25 years, the **Intercollegiate Horse Show Association** (P.O. Box 741, Stony Brook, NY 11790; 516-751-2803) has helped organize team competitions among colleges nationwide. While many of the IHSA member schools do not offer equine studies programs, they offer the opportunity to continue riding while you earn a degree that will enable you to find a job working indirectly with horses in the industry. Members do not need to own a horse to participate in the program.

Schools with Intercollegiate Horse Show Programs

ZONE 1
Connecticut, Massachusetts, New Hampshire, Rhode Island, Vermont
Region 1
Brown University, Providence, RI 02912
Connecticut College, New London, CT 06320
Johnson & Wales College, Providence, RI 02903
Rhode Island Community College, Warwick, RI 02886
Roger Williams College, Providence, RI 20809
Salve Regina, Newport, RI 02840
Stonehill College, Raynham, MA 02767
Teikyo–Post University, Waterbury, CT 06708
Trinity College, Hartford, CT 06106
University of Connecticut, Storrs, CT 06268
University of Massachusetts-Dartmouth, Dartmouth, MA 02747
University of Rhode Island, Kingston, RD 02881
Wesleyan University, Middletown, CT 06457
Wheaton College, Norton, MA 02766
Region 2
Boston University, Chestnut Hill, MA 02167
Colby–Sawyer College, New London, NH 03257
Dartmouth College, Hanover, NH 03755
Framingham State College, Framingham, MA 01701
Harvard University, Cambridge, MA 02138
Middlebury College, Middlebury, VT 05753
Mt. Ida College, Newton Centre, MA 02159
New England College, Henniker, NH 03242
Tufts University, Medford, MA 02155

University of Lowell, Lowell, MA 01854
University of New Hampshire, Durham, NH 03824
University of Vermont, Burlington, VT 05405
Region 3
American International College, Springfield, MA 01109
Amherst College, Amherst, MA 01102
Becker College, Leicester, MA 01524
Clark University, Worcester, MA 01610
College of Holy Cross, Worcester, MA 01610
Elms College, Chicopee, MA 01013
Hampshire College, Amherst, MA 01002
Landmark College, Putney, VT 05346
Mount Holyoke College, South Hadley, MA 01075
Smith College, Northampton, MA 01063
Springfield College, Springfield, MA 01109
University of Massachusetts, Amherst, MA 01003
Westfield State College, Westfield, MA 01085
Williams College, Williamstown, MA 01267
Worcester State College, Worcester, MA 01602

ZONE 2
Upstate New York, Westchester, New York City, Northern New Jersey, Canada
Region 1
Centenary College, Hackettstown, NJ 07840
College of St. Elizabeth, Convent Station, NJ 07961
Columbia-Barnard, New York, NY 10027
Cooper Union, New York, NY 10003
Drew University, Madison, NJ 07940
Fairleigh Dickinson University–Madison, Madisoin, NJ 07940
Fairleigh Dickinson University–Teaneck, Teaneck, NJ 07666
Fordham University, New York, NY 10023
Manhattanville College, Purchase, NY 10577
Marist College, Poughkeepsie, NY 12601
Marymount College, Tarrytown, NY 10591
New York University, New York, NY 10012
Pace University, New York, NY 10038
Sarah Lawrence College, Bronxville, NY 10708
United States Military Academy, West Point, NY 10996
Vassar College, Poughkeepsie, NY 12601
William Paterson College, Wayne, NJ 07470

Region 2
Alfred University, Alfred, NY 14802
Cazenovia College, Cazenovia, NY 130365
Clarkson University, Potsdam, NY 13676
Cornell University, Ithaca, NY 14850
Hamilton College, Clinton, NY 13323
Rennselaer Polytechnic Institute, Troy, NY 12181
Sienna College, Loudonville, NY 12211
Skidmore College, Saratoga Springs, NY 12866
St. Lawrence University, Canton, NY 13617
SUNY Albany, Albany, NY 12222
SUNY Binghamton, Binghamton, NY 13901
SUNY College of Tech., Canton, NY 13617
SUNY Geneseo, Geneseo, NY 14454
SUNY Morrisville, Morrisville, NY 13408
SUNY Oswego, Oswego, NY 13126
SUNY Postdam, Postdam, NY 13676
Syracuse University, Syracuse, NY 13210
University of Rochester, Rochester, NY 14627

ZONE 3
Southern Connecticut, Delaware, Long Island, Pennsylvania, Southern
New Jersey
Region 1
Adelphi University, Garden City, NY 11530
Long Island University–C.W. Post College, Brookville, NY 11548
Fairfield University, Fairfield, CT 06430
Hofstra University, Hempstead, NY 11550
Molloy College, Rockville Centre, NY 11570
Nassau Community College, Garden City, NY 11530
Sacred Heart University, Fairfield, CT 06430
St. John's University, Jamaica, NY 11439
St. Joseph's College, Brooklyn, NY 11205
Suffolk Community College, Boston, MA 02114
University of New York–Stony Brook, Stony Brook, NY 11790
Yale University, New Haven, CT 06520
Region 2
Beaver College, Glenside, PA 19038
Bucks County Community College, Newtown, PA 18940
Cedar Crest College, Allentown, PA 18104
Delaware Valley College, Doylestown, PA 18901
Kutztown University, Kutztown, PA 19530

Lehigh University, Bethlehem, PA 18015
Moravian College, Bethlehem, PA 18018
Princeton University, Princeton, NJ 08544
Rider College, Larenceville, NJ 08648
Rutgers University, New Brunswick, NJ 08903
Temple University, Philadelphia, PA 19122
University of Delaware, Newark, DE 19716
University of Pennsylvania, Philadelphia, PA 19104
West Chester University, West Chester, PA 19383

Region 3
Bucknell University, Lewisburg, PA 17837
Indiana University of Pennsylvania, Indiana, PA 15705
Pennsylvania State University, University Park, PA 16802
Seton Hall College, South Orange, NJ 07079
University of Pittsburgh, Pittsburgh, PA 15620
University of Scranton, Scranton, PA 18510
Westminster College, New Wilmington, PA 16142
West Virginia University, Morgantown, WV 26506
Wilson College, Chambersburg, PA 17201

ZONE 4
District of Columbia, Maryland, North Carolina, Virginia
Region 1
American University, Washington, DC 20016
Christopher Newport College, Newport News, VA 23606
College of William and Mary, Williamsburg, VA 23185
Georgetown University, Washington, DC 20057
Goucher College, Towson, MD 21204
Longwood College, Farmsville, VA 23901
Lynchburg College, Lynchburg, VA 24501
Mary Washington College, Fredericksburg, VA 22401
Randolph Macon Women's College, Lynchburg, VA 24503
Sweet Briar College, Sweet Briar, VA 24595
Towson State University, Towson, MD 21204
University of Maryland, College Park, MD 20742
University of Richmond, Richmond, VA 23173
University of Virginia, Charlottesville, VA 22906

Region 2
Averett College, Danville, VA 24541
Duke University, Durham, NC 27706
Ferrum College, Ferrum, VA 24088
Hollins College, Hollins College, VA 24020

Martin Community College, Williamston, NC 27892
North Carolina State University, Raleigh, NC 27650
Queens College, Charlotte, NC 28274
Radford University, Radford, VA 24142
St. Andrews Presbyterian College, Laurinburg, NC 28352
Southern Virginia College, Buena Vista, VA 22906
University of North Carolina–Chapel Hill, Chapel Hill, NC 27514
Virginia Intermont College, Bristol, VA 24201
Virginia Polytechnic Institute and State University, Blacksburg,
    VA 24061

ZONE 5
*Alabama, Florida, Georgia, Kentucky, Louisiana, Mississippi, Missouri,
South Carolina, Southern Illinois, Tennessee*
<u>Region 1</u>
Hiwassee College, Madisonville, TN 37354
Midway College, Midway, KY 40347
Maryville College, St. Louis, MO 63141
Morehead State University, Morehead, KY 40351
Pellissippi State Technical College, Knoxville, TN 37933
Tennessee Tech University, Cookeville, TN 38501
University of Kentucky, Lexington, KY 40506
University of Louisville, Louisville, KY 40208
University of the South, Sewanee, TN 37375
University of Tennessee, Knoxville, TN 37919
<u>Region 2</u>
Berry College, Mount Berry, GA 30149
Clemson University, Clemson, SC 29631
College of Charleston, Charleston, SC 29401
Converse College, Spartanburg, SC 29301
Erskine College, Due West, SC 29639
Florida State University, Tallahassee, FL 32306
Georgia Southern University, Atlanta, GA 30303
University of Alabama, University, AL 35486
University of Florida, Gainesville, FL 32611
University of Georgia, Athens, GA 30602
University of South Carolina, Columbia, SC 29208
Wesleyan College, Macon, GA 31297
<u>Region 3</u>
John A. Logan College, Carterville, IL 62918
Middle Tennessee State University, Murfreesboro, TN 37132
Murray State University, Murray, KY 42071

Northeast Missouri State University, Kirksville, MO 63501
Rhodes College, Memphis, TN 38112
Southern Illinois University, Carbondale, IL 62901
Southwest Missouri State University, Cape Girardeau, MO 63701
University of Memphis, Memphis, TN 38152
Vanderbilt University, Nashville, TN 37212
Western Kentucky University, Bowling Green, 42101

ZONE 6
*Illinois, Indiana, Iowa, Kansas, Michigan, Ohio, West Virginia,
Wisconsin*
<u>Region 1</u>
Columbus State Community College, Columbus, OH 43216
Hiram College, Hiram, OH 44234
Kent State University, Kent, OH 44242
Lake Erie College, Painesville, OH 44077
Miami University of Ohio, Oxford, OH 43056
Oberlin College, Oberlin, OH 44074
Ohio State University, Columbus, OH 43210
Ohio University, Athens, OH 45701
Salem Teikyo University, Salem, WV 26426
University of Cincinnati, Cincinati, OH 45221
<u>Region 2</u>
Anderson College, Anderson, IN 46011
Ball State University, Muncie, IN 47306
Earlham College, Richmond, IN 47374
Indiana University–Purdue University at Indianapolis, Indianapo-
    lis, IN 46202
Indiana University, Bloomington, IN 47405
Iowa State University, Ames, IA 50011
Northwestern University, Evanston, IL 60201
Parkland College, Champaign, IL 61820
Purdue University, West Lafayette, IN 47907
St. Mary's of the Woods College, St. Mary-of-the-Woods, IN
    47876
Taylor University, Upland, IN 46989
University of Illinois, Urbana, IL 61801
University of Minnesota–Crookston, Crookston, MN 56716
University of Notre Dame, Notre Dame, IN 46556
<u>Region 3</u>
Hillsdale College, Hillsdale, MI 49242
Michigan State University, East Lansing, MI 48824

Ohio Wesleyan University, Delaware, OH 43015
Otterbein College, Westerville, OH 43081
University of Findlay, Findlay, OH 45840
University of Michigan, Ann Arbor, MI 48109
Western Michigan University, Kalamazoo, MI 49008

ZONE 7
Colorado, Kansas, Louisiana, New Mexico, Oklahoma, Texas,
Wyoming
Region 1
Colby Community College, Colby, KS 67701
Colorado State University, Fort Collins, CO 80523
Laramie County Community College, Cheyenne, WY 82001
New Mexico State University, Las Cruces, NM 88003
United States Air Force Academy, USAFA, CO 80840
University of Colorado, Boulder, CO 80309
University of Denver, Denver, CO 80208
University of Wyoming, Laramie, WY 82071
Region 2
Northwestern State University of Louisiana, Natchitches,
    LA 71457
Oklahoma State University, Stillwater, OK 74078
Sul Ross University, Alpine, TX 79830
Tarleton State University, Stephenville, TX 76402
Texas A&M University, College Staion, TX 77843
Texas Tech University, Lubbock, TX 79409
University of Texas–Austin, Austin, TX 78712
West Texas A&M University, Canyon, TX 79016

ZONE 8
California, Nevada, Oregon
Cal Poly State University–Pomona, Pomona, CA 91768
Cal Poly State University–San Luis Obispo, San Luis Obispo,
    CA 93407
California State University–Fresno, Fresno, CA 93740
College of the Sequoias, Visalia, CA 93277
Stanford University, Stanford, CA 94305
University of California–Davis, Davis, CA 95616
University of California–San Diego, La Jolla, CA 92093
University of Nevada–Reno, Reno, NV 89557
University of Oregon, Eugene, OR 97403
University of Southern California, Los Angeles, CA 90007

The **National Intercollegiate Rodeo Association** (1815 Portland Ave., #3, Walla Walla, WA 99362-2246; 509-529-4402) sanctions over 100 rodeos annually for students enrolled at U.S. colleges and universities. Like the IHSA, some of the NIRA programs are located at schools that do not offer equine studies programs, and horse ownership is not a prerequisite for participation.

SCHOOLS WITH INTERCOLLEGIATE RODEO PROGRAMS

BIG SKY REGION
Blackfeet Community College, Browning, MT 59417
Montana State University, Bozeman, MT 59717
UMT/School of Journalism, Missoula, MT 59812
Dawson Community College, Glendive, MT 59330
Northern Montana College, Havre, MT 59501
Western Montana College, Dillon, MT 59725
Miles Community College, Miles City, MT 59301
Northwest College, Powell, WY 82435

CENTRAL PLAINS REGION
Colby Community College, Colby, KS 67701
Fort Hays State University, Hays, KS 67601-4099
Kansas State University, Manhattan, KS 66502
Connors State College, Warner, OK 74469
Fort Scott Community College, Fort Scott, KS 66701
Murray State College, Tishomingo, OK 73460
Dodge City Community College, Dodge City, KS 67801-2399
Garden City Community College, Garden City, KS 67846
Northeastern Oklahoma A&M College, Miami, OK 74354
Northwest Missouri State University, Maryville, MO 64468-6001
Panhandle State University, Goodwell, OK 73939-0280
Southwestern Oklahoma State Univ., Weatherford, OK 73096
Northwestern Oklahoma State University, Alva, OK 73717-9898
Pratt Community College, Pratt, KS 67124
Western Oklahoma State College, Altus, OK 73521
Oklahoma State University, Stillwater, OK 74078-0107
Southeastern Oklahoma State University, Durant, OK 74701

CENTRAL ROCKY MOUNTAIN REGION
Casper College, Casper, WY 82601
Colorado State University, Fort Collins, CO 80523
Laramie County Community College, Cheyenne, WY 82007

Central Wyoming College, Riverton, WY 82501
Eastern Wyoming College, Torrington, WY 82240
Mesa State College, Grand Junction, CO 81501
Chadron State College, Chadron, NE 69337
Lamar Community College, Lamar, CO 81052
Northeastern Junior College, Sterling, CO 80751
Sheridan College, Sheridan, WY 82801
University of Southern Colorado, Pueblo, CO 81001
University of Wyoming, Laramie, WY 82071
University of Colorado, Boulder, CO 80309-0355

GRAND CANYON REGION
Central Arizona College, Coolidge, AZ 85228
New Mexico State University, Las Cruces, NM 88003
San Juan College, Farmington, NM 87402
University of Nevada–Las Vegas, Las Vegas, NV 89154-0026
Cochise Community College, Douglas, AZ 85607
Northern Arizona University, Flagstaff, AZ 86001
Scottsdale Community College, Scottsdale, AZ 85251
Western New Mexico University, Silver City, NM 88062
Navajo Community College, Tsaile, AZ 86556
Pima Community College, Tucson, AZ 85741
University of Arizona, Tucson, AZ 85721

GREAT PLAINS REGION
Black Hills State University, Spearfish, SD 57799-9535
Lake Area Technical Institute, Watertown, SD 57201-0730
North Dakota State University, Fargo, ND 58105
University of Nebraska–Lincoln, Lincoln, NE 68583-0922
Dickinson State University, Dickinson, ND 58601
Mitchell Technical Institute, Mitchell, SD 57301
South Dakota State University, Brookings, SD 57007
University of Wisconsin–River Falls, River Falls, WI 54022
Iowa State University, Ames, IA 50011
Nebraska College of Technical AG, Curtis, NE 69025-0069
Southwestern Community College, Creston, IA 50801
Western Dakota Technical Institute, Rapid City, SD 57701

NORTHWEST REGION
Blue Mountain Community College, Pendleton, OR 97801
Lewis-Clark State College, Clarkston, WA 99403
Columbia Basin College, Pasco, WA 99301

Treasure Valley Community College, Ontario, OR 97914
Eastern Oregon State College, Lagrande, OR 97850
University of Idaho, Moscow, ID 83844-2330
Walla Walla Community College, Walla Walla, WA 99362
Washington State University, Pullman, WA 99164-6210

OZARK REGION
Missouri Valley College, Marshall, MO 65340
Southern Arkansas University, McNell, AR 71752
University of Tennessee–Martin, Martin, TN 38238
Livingston University, Livingston, AL 35470
Murray State University, Murray, KY 42071
Southwest Missouri State University, Springfield, MO 65804
Michigan State University, East Lansing, MI 48824
Northwest Mississippi Community College, Senatobia, MS 38668
University of Missouri–Columbia, Columbia, MO 65201

ROCKY MOUNTAIN REGION
Boise State University, Boise, ID 83725
College of Eastern Utah, Price, UT 84501
College of Southern Idaho, Twin Falls, ID 83301
Dixie College, St. George, UT 84770
Ricks College, Rexburg, ID 83440
Utah Valley State College, Orem, UT 84058
Idaho State University, Pocatello, ID 83209
Southern Utah University, Cedar City, UT 84720
Weber State University, Ogden, UT 84408-3001
Northern Nevada Community College, Elko, NV 89801
Utah State University, Logan, UT 84322-2300

SOUTHERN REGION
Angelina College, Lufkin, TX 75902
North Central Texas College, Gainesville, TX 76240-4699
Sam Houston State University, Huntsville, TX 77341-2088
Hill College, Hillsboro, TX 76645
Northeast Texas Community College, Mt. Pleasant, TX 75456
Southwest Texas Junior College, Uvalde, TX 78801
McNeese State University, Lake Charles, LA 70609
Northwestern State University, Natchitoches, LA 71497
Southwest Texas State University, San Marcos, TX 78666
Stephen F. Austin State University, Nacogdoches, TX 75962
Trinity Valley Community College, Athens, TX 75751

Tyler Junior College, Tyler, TX 75711
Texas A&M University–Kingsville, Kingsville, TX 78363
Wharton County Junior College, Wharton, TX 77488

SOUTHWEST REGION
Cisco Junior College, Cisco, Texas 76437
Hardin-Simmons University, Abilene, TX 79698
Odessa College, Odessa, TX 79764
Texas Technical University–Lubbock, Lubbock, TX 79409
Eastern New Mexico University, Portales, NM 88130
Howard County Junior College, Big Spring, TX 79720
Sul Ross State University, Alpine, TX 79832
Vernon Regional Junior College, Vernon, TX 76384
Frank Phillips College, Borger, TX 79008-5118
New Mexico Junior College, Hobbs, NM 88240
Tarleton State University, Stephenville, TX 76402
Weatherford College, Weatherford, TX 76086
West Texas A&M University, Canyon, TX 79016
Western Texas College, Snyder, TX 79549

WEST COAST REGION
Cal Poly State University–San Luis Obispo, San Luis Obispo,
   CA 93401
Pierce College, Woodland Hills, CA 91371
California State University, Prather, CA 93651
West Hills College, Coalinga, CA 93210
Lassen College, Susanville, CA 96130

FUNDING AN EQUINE EDUCATION

Marshalling the financial resources for an education often requires considerable research to find potential sources of funds and to determine if you qualify for them. High school guidance offices and the directors of financial aid at trade schools and colleges can help you determine if federal aid in the form of Pell Grants, Federal Stafford Loans, Federal Plus Loans, or Federal Supplemental Loans is available to you. Those with military service can contact a local Veterans Administration office to see how they can take advantage of GI loans to finance their career.

Financially eligible students enrolled in equine-related degree courses may be able to take advantage of federal work-study programs that will not only help them pay for their education but also give them some work experience to put on their resumes. Jobs around university-maintained barns might include anything from cleaning stalls to staying up with mares due to foal. Univer-

Besides the income and sheer pleasure of contact with horses, working as a groom provides a diversity of valuable experiences.

sity research labs and veterinary clinics also use work-study students for many jobs that offer an opportunity to earn money, gain experience, and observe firsthand how established professionals go about their jobs. There are only a limited number of these jobs available at even the largest schools. Inquire about equine-career-related work-study opportunities at particular schools early in the search process if it is important.

Equine program students seeking scholarships should discuss every possibility with their high school guidance counselor and the financial aid directors of schools they apply to. Different states, towns, and schools have unique scholarship opportunities you should explore. Within the equine industry, a number of groups offer small scholarships to help defray expenses for students pursuing equine-related careers. In addition to having academic and other qualifications, most of these scholarships are restricted to active members of the sponsoring organization, those aiming at specific careers, or those studying at particular schools. If you meet the often very narrow eligibility requirements, it can be worthwhile to apply. Among the sponsoring organizations are:

American Association of Equine Practitioners
4075 Iron Works Pike, Lexington, KY 40511; 606-233-0147
Six $1,500 scholarships for fourth-year veterinary students; $1,000 scholarship to current or graduate member of the United States Pony Club who is also a student member of AAEP

American Morgan Horse Institute
P.O. Box 519; Shelburne, VT 05482; 802-985-8477
Two $1,500 and $1,250 scholarships for members of the American Morgan Horse Association Junior Youth Programs

American Paint Horse Association
P.O. Box 961023, Fort Worth, TX 76161-0023; 817-439-3400
Scholarships from $750 to $1,000 for vocational or degree studies for youth members of the American Paint Horse Association

American Quarter Horse Association
P.O. Box 200, Amarillo, TX 79168; 806-376-4811
Several scholarships of $1,000 or less for members of the American Junior Quarter Horse Association for 2 years or more

Appaloosa Horse Club, Inc.
Box 8403, Moscow, ID 83843; 208-882-5578
Eight $1,000 scholarships for youth members of the Appaloosa Horse Club, Inc.

Dude Ranchers Educational Trust
P.O. Box G471, La Porte, CO 80535-0471; 303-223-8440
Single $500 scholarship to a school in any of twelve Western states or Canadian provinces for students studying business skills and agreeing to work the guest season at a member dude ranch

Harness Horse Youth Foundation
14950 Greyhound Ct, Suite 210, Carmel, IN 46032;
317-848-5132
Up to $20,000 in scholarship funds available to students pursuing a careeer in the horse industry

Harness Tracks of America, Inc.
4640 East Sunrise, Suite 200, Tuscon, AZ 85718-4576;
602-529-2525
Up to $15,000 in scholarships available to children of those actively involved in harness racing

Intercollegiate Horse Show Association
Hollow Rd., Box 741, Stony Brook, NY 11790; 914-773-3788
Scholarships of up to $500 available to members of intercollegiate riding teams

International Arabian Horse Association
P.O. Box 33696, Denver, CO 80233-0696; 303-450-4774
More than eighty $500 scholarships available to winners in the IAHA National Judging Contest, Youth National Champions, and other youth pursuing horse careers

National 4-H Clubs
Contact your state 4-H office of the National 4-H Council, 7100 Connecticut Ave., Chevy Chase, MD 20815-4999; 301-961-2830

National Show Horse Registry
10401 Linn Station Rd., Suite 237, Louisville, KY 40233;
502-423-1902
Up to $5,000 in scholarship funds available to the top ten equitation winners at the National Championship Horse Show

Pony of the Americas Club, Inc.
5240 Elmwood Ave., Indianapolis, IN 46203-5990;
317-788-0107
Two scholarships of $400 or more available to members of the Pony of the Americas Club, Inc.

Professional Horseman's Association of America
20 Blue Ridge Lane, Wilton, CT 06897-4127; 203-834-0790
Scholarships of $500 to members of PHA or their children.

EDUCATION GUIDES

There are several publications that provide detailed information about colleges and universities that offer degrees in equine studies or related fields such as animal science or veterinary medicine. They can also lead you to schools that offer riding activities and horse competitions even though they do not offer equine-related degrees.

Equine Educational Programs Directory
(Dr. Sue Stuska, Martin Community College, 1161 Kehukee Park Rd., Williamston, NC 27892-9988; 919-972-1521; $17.95 postpaid)

This directory has the most complete listing of trade schools, colleges, and universities in the United States offering not only equine studies courses but also related courses such as animal husbandry, pre-vet and veterinary medicine, and farrier science. Each entry is coded to indicate which degrees are offered, what riding styles or breeds are emphasized, whether the college has riding clubs or student competitions, and the type of riding or boarding facilities available. Contact names, addresses, and phone numbers get you to the person who can tell you more.

Equine School and College Directory
(Harness Horse Youth Foundation, Inc., 14950 Greyhound Court, Suite 210, Carmel, IN 46032; 317-848-5132; $5.00)

This book gives thumbnail sketches of approximately 100 colleges and universities with degrees that relate to horses, with an emphasis on those dealing with racehorses. In addition to degrees, each description offers information about courses, facilities, internships, and job placement. This directory also offers a listing of over three dozen scholarships ranging from a few hundred to several thousand dollars each offered for those pursing equine studies.

Guide to Equine Employment and Education
(Whitehouse Publishing, P.O. Box 1778, Vernon, B.C., V1T 8C3, Canada; 604-545-9896; $35 plus postage and handling)

This guide lists the names and addresses of secondary schools, trade schools, colleges, and universities—not only in North America but worldwide—with some kind of riding program or equestrian degree. The listings are not coded by degrees or riding specialties, so you will have to do your own research to find out what programs each school offers; but if you want to broaden your job horizons and think globally, this book can help. This publication also offers concise information about getting a job, including lists of possible industry contacts.

Manning's Guide to Colleges and Secondary Equestrian Programs (Manning Associates, 69 Taylor Road, Shelburne, MA 01370; $15.95 postpaid)

This guide lists secondary schools (ninth through twelfth grades) and colleges offering either equine degrees and riding programs or only riding programs, with an emphasis on schools where English-style riding prevails. In-depth profiles of over two dozen schools provide good comparisons for those weighing their educational options.

CAREER CLOSE-UP

VETERINARIAN

Dr. Ron Gaeta adjusts his baseball cap and once again checks the assortment of vaccines and medications he is carrying before he opens the door of his truck. Later today he will use these to help some sick horses improve and some healthy horses stay that way. Today's first stop, however, is not the kind budding veterinarians dream of when they envision helping and saving horses. Despite the application of all his medical skills, a colic case slipped away last night. This morning will start with an autopsy. Would surgery have saved the horse, or was the ailment that would not respond to pharmaceutical treatment beyond surgical intervention as well? Armed with the answer, he may be better able to help the next horse with similar symptoms.

Ron Gaeta grew up with horses. An active Pony Clubber, he played polo, fox hunted, and competed in hunter-jumper events while in high school. At the same time, he also began to think about his future and plan a career. In the "try before you buy" tradition of thousands of youngsters before him, he sought out part-time work with a veterinarian to see if he was cut out for a medical destiny. One summer was spent with an equine dentist. Without exception, practicing veterinarians and veterinary schools recommend that youngsters interested in veterinary careers get practical experience before they apply to vet school. Not only does working for a vet show seriousness of purpose to an application committee, it also quickly sorts out those who will be unable to take the grisly side of the profession from those who see only the pleasant aspects. "Start early, do a lot of volunteer work, even take non-paid summer jobs," he advises. While small-animal vets sometimes hire youngsters to work in their clinics, equine vets basically work on the road out of their trucks. Paying jobs as "assistants" are not the norm.

Veterinary school is basically a four-year graduate program. Applicants first take pre-veterinary courses, which may be specially designed programs leading to veterinary school or related degrees such as animal science. Good grades and extracurricular activities related to animal science or veterinary science can all influence application committees when there are more applicants than openings. Graduate veterinarians typically become associates with established practices. After several years, they may be invited to become a partner or a part-owner of the practice.

Gaeta points out that vets need to acquire business skills as well as medical skills, since a veterinary practice is actually a small business. As much as 20 percent of a vet's time may be spent on business paperwork and things such as personnel management that all small businesses must deal with. School is never over. There are always professional journals to keep up with and symposiums to attend. There is no such thing as a "typical" day. The day may begin with a farm call to do routine vaccinations, be interrupted by an emergency surgery, and end with a late-night foaling. Boredom is one thing veterinarians do not worry about.

Today as Dr. Gaeta turns his truck down a gravel lane toward the field where a hole has already been dug for burying the colic victim, he is accompanied by his veterinary technician and a young lady who wants to become a vet and has asked to ride along to observe. She has never seen an autopsy. As Dr. Gaeta proceeds, he keeps an eye on her but there is no squeamishness, only intense curiosity. So he takes time to explain everything he sees and describe how the internal organs function. This time, he determines, surgery would not have saved the horse or even given him a little more time. But what he has learned this morning may be helpful tomorrow. And what a future veterinarian has seen may help her save a horse in years to come. ∎

Chapter 4

Getting Experience

The mix of education and experience you will need to be an irresistible job candidate will vary a great deal depending on your career goal. For careers working directly with horses in areas such as farm management, horse transportation, training or riding instruction, you can never have too much hands-on experience. In jobs such as sales, retailing, insurance, or construction, the more people know about horses and the horse industry, the more they will be able to understand their customers' needs. However, the number of times they have perfectly applied a standing bandage or attended a foaling will not significantly affect their job potential one way or the other. Jobs like pedigree analysis, blood typing, or custom embroidery do not require any hands-on horse experience at all.

We have already mentioned the heavy emphasis many horsemen put on experience when hiring people for jobs working directly with horses. That may seem unfair if your circumstances allowed only a few years of riding lessons while your competition was growing up on a breeding farm or the show circuit. This is where planning comes in. If your heart is set on a specific career goal, you need to find out how much prior experience is expected of people in that job. (Remember that list of people you were going to call in Chapter 2?) The alternative is to set your sights on a career that suits your existing experience level.

WHILE YOU ARE IN HIGH SCHOOL

It is never too soon to start building the experience side of your resume. Experience can include a wide range of activities such as caring for your own or someone else's horses, horse shows or other competitions you participate in actively, volunteering at a veterinary clinic, and weekend or summer jobs working for other horsemen.

Potential employers look for different kinds of experience, so everything you have done with horses may not necessarily impress every future employer. Your walls might be lined with colorful show ribbons earned in equitation classes, but your future employer might be less impressed by the ribbon count than by the fact that you were responsible for the complete care and conditioning of your own horse. Horse care is a very different kind of experience from that of the rider who just shows up at the barn and takes the reins from the trainer's hand. Jobs that prove your ability to consistently follow through on repetitive daily chores that are part of managing a horse facility may be more impressive to some employers than excellent riding skills.

Participation in youth activities such as 4-H, Pony Club, the American Junior Quarter Horse Association, and other association-sponsored youth groups also counts as horse experience. Pony Club's program, for example, defines riding and horse skills at a progression of levels. Your current rating tells a potential employer exactly what level of stable and riding skills you are qualified for.

One excellent way to learn a lot about horses is to spend time observing a top equine professional at work. How do you convince a busy professional that it is worth his or her while to let you hang around the barn?

Approach them with a simple but businesslike proposal on three sheets of paper.

THE FIRST SHEET should be a short resume. It does not have to be as detailed as a job resume (see Chapter 5) but it should include:

- ✍ Your name, address, and phone number (the name of your parents and their addresses and phone numbers if different from yours)
- ✍ Where you are enrolled in school and what your current grade level is
- ✍ Any current horse experience you have such as owning a horse, taking riding lessons, competing, or participating in 4-H, Pony Club, or a breed youth club
- ✍ Your horse-career goal.

THE SECOND PAGE should contain two short paragraphs:

- ✍ The first one, "What I Would Like to Learn," should describe why you want to observe the professional at work. Learning more about horse care, training techniques, or an entirely new skill, such as driving, might be your primary interest. Do not expect free riding, especially at a barn full of young horses in training or expensive show horses belonging to the professional's clients.
- ✍ The second paragraph, "What I Can Contribute," should describe what you are willing to contribute in return for the opportunity to listen, watch, and learn from someone really good. That might be help with stall cleaning, tack care, scrubbing water buckets, or sweeping aisles and cobwebs. These paragraphs tell the professional right up front what your expectations are and whether you are more likely to be a nuisance or a help around the barn. In writing both of your paragraphs, be realistic about how much time you have available and when those hours are free.

THE THIRD SHEET OF PAPER, if you are under 18, should be a note from your parents indicating that they understand you are making this request and that you have their approval. Professionals who do not run public lesson stables or training barns may not have insurance that will cover them if you are hurt while working with their horses. They may want to talk to your parents about a liability release and this note indicates your parents' will-

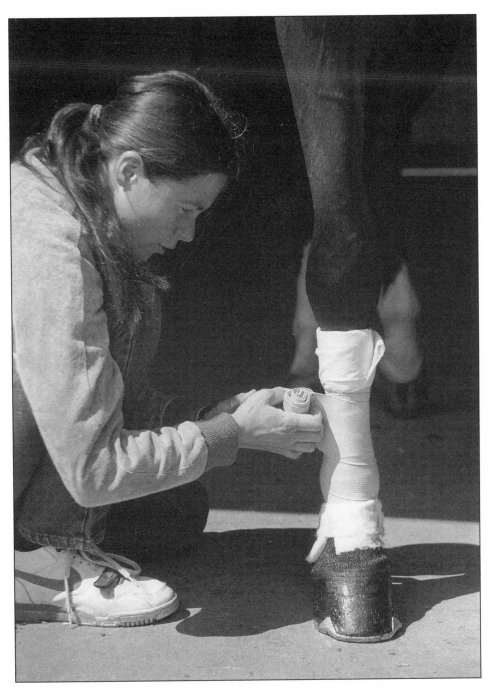

Employers are impressed by your ability to take complete responsibility for a horse's care. Daily chores are just as important as excellent riding skills.

ingness to open a dialog.

Put your three sheets of paper into a folder with pockets from a stationery store. If you have a photo of yourself with your horse, you might include that, too, or a quality photocopy. Call ahead to be sure the professional will be in and ask if you can drop off your folder. When you do, shake hands firmly and make eye contact as you explain you are looking for more experience in the horse industry to help you meet a career goal and that you would like him or her to look at a short proposal. Leave your folder and make an appointment to pick it up again at a later date ("I'll come back next Tuesday . . .") so you can request an answer.

If the answer is "no," ask the professional to recommend other places where you might get more experience. Try to leave with at least two other names, and politely thank the professional for considering your request. The horse world is a small one, and you can bet you will meet that professional again down the road some day. Leave a good impression.

Students interested in veterinary medicine often gain experience by volunteering time at a veterinary hospital near them and accompanying a veterinarian on his or her rounds. Most veterinary schools expect this kind of experience on the application of any serious candidate. Get to know the equine veterinarians in your area. Like people doctors, some equine vets specialize. One doctor's practice may be predominantly racehorses, another may deal primarily with backyard pleasure horses, and still another may be emphasizing alternative therapies like chiropracty and acupuncture. Prepare your three-sheet proposal and approach a vet whose practice is similar to the kind of veterinary medicine you see yourself practicing some day.

Even though you may eventually be asked to take on some real responsibility at a professional facility or veterinary hospital, don't expect to be paid for an informal apprenticeship or internship (depending on your age and the state you live in, it might even be illegal for you to work for pay or for more than a certain number of hours). If that seems unfair, remember that you are asking a busy, established professional to give you free training—training that will take the person's time away from income-earning business activities. You pay no tuition and the professional pays no wages.

BEYOND HIGH SCHOOL

Colleges with equine studies programs understand the importance of having hands-on horse experience. For their students approaching graduation, many arrange formal internships that may last a few weeks or as long as a semester. You should inquire about these programs as part of any college selection process.

Find out how long the internships are. While a semester-long internship can give you current work experience to cite when you start applying for jobs after graduation, don't expect an internship of a few weeks to make up for years of little or no hands-on experience. Find out whether internships are available to all students or only to some. Also find out where the internships will be. An internship on a broodmare farm may not be extremely useful if you intend to teach riding after graduation. Similarly, if you spend a semester as a riding teacher's assistant when you really hope to land a job at a Thoroughbred farm as a stallion manager, your experience will not be as meaningful to potential employers. While any experience adds to your knowledge and skills, the closer the internship comes to meshing with your career goals, the better it will be when you start your job hunt. Any experience, of course, may be useful somewhere down the line.

Active participation in school-sponsored riding activities or animal science clubs is another way to beef up the experience side of your resume during your college years. Working as a show secretary, planning a field trip, or handling publicity for a club event shows prospective employers that you are organized and can work well with the public. Intercollegiate polo, horse show, and rodeo programs can demonstrate sportsmanship and an ability to cooperate on a team. If you assume a leadership role in a student riding club or organizations like the Block & Bridle Clubs found on many campuses with animal science programs, you also add important nonhorse skills to your resume.

GETTING PAID WHILE YOU GET EXPERIENCE

Working student programs are a tool with which those who opt to skip college can make their way into the horse industry. At its simplest, the concept of a "working student" is someone who exchanges labor for lessons with a professional. Few arrangements in the horse industry seem to cause more rancor than these working-student agreements, however. Why? The primary reasons are mismatched expectations and failure to put each person's expectations into writing right from the start.

You could consider the working student an older, more mature extension of our high school student who asked to hang around the barn and learn everything he or she could. In reality, working-student arrangements are usually far more complex both economically and psychologically. Since the primary benefit to a working student is not monetary compensation but the opportunity to learn from someone at the top of his or her profession, it is important to be sure the professional is of the highest caliber.

Working students generally live at the professional's farm, with housing and sometimes utilities provided. Board for a student's horse is often included in the arrangement, along with free lessons. There is usually a very small wage paid weekly, and the employer may or may not include health insurance in the deal. In exchange for all of this, the student agrees to work for the professional, helping with stable management and horse care, and perhaps functioning as an assistant instructor or trainer from time to time as he or she gains experience.

The problem with too many working-student relationships is that both the student and the professional wind up feeling exploited. Let us say that the professional charges $100 per lesson and $600 monthly for training board, and that our working student is getting two lessons per week. She is also being paid $200

per week plus receiving housing worth $250 a month in that geographic area (assume that four working students share a four-bedroom house in the Northeast, which the professional could rent for $1000 monthly—housing values vary widely throughout the country). From the professional's standpoint, the working student costs him approximately $2,450 monthly, not counting the value that should be placed on the intangible benefit of working daily alongside a top person in the field. Enjoying the opportunity to network with his contacts as well as soaking up the techniques and practices that amount to his "trade secrets" has to be worth a great deal, he reckons.

Our working student, however, never sees any cash except the weekly $200. She also sees that she is working 12-hour days or better, often at menial and somewhat redundant tasks. After awhile, sharing bathrooms and refrigerators with several other people begins to lose its appeal. She computes her hourly wage based on her weekly cash wages, discovers she could be making more flipping hamburgers, and begins to feel under-appreciated. The professional may fail to be diligent about scheduling the working student's lesson time or fulfilling other promises made before the student arrived. In the eyes of the student, her shiny professional hero and his sterling reputation begin to tarnish.

The best way to avoid these problems is to put everything in writing. At a minimum, you should write the professional a letter outlining any verbal agreement you have made. If you feel that you risk losing the working student position by writing an agreement letter, the arrangement is probably not worth making. Any businesslike professional will understand the value of clarifying everyone's expectations and any verbal agreements on paper.

YOUR WRITTEN AGREEMENT should include:

- ✍ What your duties will be at the professional's barn. The professional should try to be as realistic as possible when developing this list. However, to provide the flexibility that the horse industry demands, he might include a phrase such as "and other duties as assigned," which gives him the right to change the duty list to meet future needs that can't be anticipated right now.

- ✍ Working conditions, including things like days on and days off, the facility's dress code, how the competition season will affect work schedules, etc. The idea here is to be sure everyone is clear about potential problems up front and that reasonable provision is made to keep them from blowing up into problems. For example, anyone working directly with horses has to understand that truly regular hours are almost impossible to set. Working three weeks straight without a day off, for example, would be an undue burden unless you have an agreement in advance that during foaling season you agree to be on-call twenty-four hours round the clock in exchange for a block of time off after all the mares have delivered.

- ✍ Your complete compensation package including housing, any utilities or insurance, board for your horse, the num-

ber of lessons you can expect and the schedule for them,
your weekly salary, and any other compensation.

✍ If board for your horse is included in your agreement,
specify what "board" covers. Students' horses may be
housed in different areas or treated differently than paying
boarders. Does board cover periodic worming? Will you
have any control over what vet or farrier you can use? Will
you be allowed to compete your horse while you are a
working student?

✍ The date on which the agreement will end or be reviewed
for renewal.

A letter outlining any verbal agreements, once written and
accepted, becomes a binding contract in most states.

While formal apprenticeships are rare in the horse industry,
occasionally an experienced tradesman agrees to take on an
employee who will learn on the job. Some farriers and saddle
makers who have tried these arrangements report dissatisfaction.
They grumble that trainees are often too impatient to spend the
necessary time to really learn a trade thoroughly. The tradesmen
sometimes find they have simply trained competitors. Many
resent that their former pupils use the apprenticeship as a marketing tool while turning out what the tradesmen consider inferior
products. They feel that their own reputations suffer as a result.

On the other side, the trainees say they feel tremendous pressure to get out and make a living. Some complain of being
exploited as cheap labor, a feeling that they are not accomplishing
anything, and a lack of clear goals. The real problem is that both
sides had expectations they did not make clear before beginning
to work together.

However informal, any apprenticeship agreement should con-
sist of more than just a handshake. These relationships can be
particularly difficult because the most gifted craftsman may be a
poor teacher, and neither side is aware of this difficulty before
they agree to work together. Problems almost always arise because
the agreements are too loosely organized and neither person is
fully aware of the other's expectations. Each party should list in as
much detail as possible what skills they expect to learn or impart,
what training benchmarks there will be along the way (perhaps
marked by wage increases), and when the training period will
end. The craftsman may want to include a "non-compete clause"
that restricts the trainee from setting up shop within a certain geo-

graphic area or for a certain time after the training is completed so he does not wind up training his competition. Similarly, an agreement may state what the terms of employment will be if the tradesman and his apprentice decide to continue their relationship after the training period.

It is a smart idea to ask a lawyer who specializes in legal business matters and is familiar with your federal and state employment laws to check over any formal working-student or apprentice agreement before you sign on the dotted line. A few hundred dollars could be very well spent if they ensure that everyone's concerns are addressed and prevent future bitterness or misunderstanding.

CERTIFICATION PROGRAMS

Certification and licensing programs offer one more way to add to your horse industry credentials. Focusing on specific skills, they involve a test or examination by qualified experts who judge whether or not you have reached a certain level of competence recognized by the certifying organization. These programs are aimed at those coming out of college and ready to enter the job market or those already in the job market who want to add to their credentials. Certification proves to the world that you really do know what you say you know. Racehorse trainers, riding instructors, farriers, massage therapists, and horse show officials all have licensing or certification programs that are described with each individual career in Chapter 7.

RIDING INSTRUCTOR

Alden Rivers grew up loving horses. His family always had horses and he rode from childhood into young adulthood. Rivers never thought to make a "name" for himself as a competitor, only to enjoy horses to their fullest for their own sake and for the emotional satisfaction of associating with horses. It seemed perfectly natural to him to skip college. Money, he determined, was not that important to him, so despite a lack of impressive credentials for a show career or an apprenticeship with a well-known professional, Alden hung out his shingle as a riding instructor. "I made a dramatic gesture," he says, "then I had to call upon all my resources and basically learn how to be an instructor on the job."

"Twenty-five years ago, we didn't have the technical knowledge about riding," he points out. The best instructors really taught by the seat of their pants. Many were excellent riders but were not very analytical about how they did what they did. They lacked the communication skills to explain their techniques to other people. "Teaching wasn't a separate skill back then."

Rivers found, however, that he had a natural talent for working with people. And he found a unique niche that no one else had filled. Many riders could not afford to board horses with their trainers, or their jobs made it difficult for them to trailer to trainers every week. To accommodate them, Rivers went to them and worked with them at home. Then he would gather his growing band at horse shows so that he could coach and encourage them as a group. His clients loved the support they enjoyed from one another, and the work-at-home, meet-at-shows arrangement was formalized into a group called the Foxtrotters after one member commented that a particular class looked like everyone was doing ballroom dancing.

Rivers' clients enjoy working with an instructor who is analytical without being overly critical. Most ride for enjoyment and to release the stress of daily life and jobs. Although

they want to improve, many are put off by professionals who become pushy or impatient with riders—particularly adult riders—who cannot be totally dedicated to show ring success. Rivers leases barn space, where he works with clients who want to board their horses. But he still maintains a strong base of backyard horsemen eager for sympathetic and supportive instruction.

If he had to do it over, however, he would start by going to college. "A career with horses involves so much more than horse knowledge," he explains. "You must know bookkeeping, record keeping, a little accounting, how to advertise, and how to communicate with people from ages 5 to 95." Rivers also recommends training in psychology for anyone contemplating a career as an instructor. "There's a lot of psychological problems with fear working with horses and you have to know how to deal with that. If you go to college, you can work on all these skills. Then if you still want to do horses, fine. But if you decide to do something else, you'll have the skills to fall back on."

Working with horses as a career often involves trade offs, Rivers point out. "The financial rewards are not there, so you must love horses and love the horse business." ■

Chapter 5

Getting Hired

If you have done your homework and planned carefully, you will reach the end of your education years with a combination of formal schooling and experience that qualify you for the career you want. Now it is time to go looking for that first job.

To present yourself to your contacts and potential employers, you need a basic set of personal marketing tools that includes a resume, a cover letter, and a business card. Later on when you reach the interview stage, you might want to add letters of reference, a photograph of yourself, or a copy of a pertinent project, depending on the kind of job you are applying for.

For starters, sit down and make a "brag list." This is not an exercise in being conceited. It is a way to paint a picture of yourself to use as you develop your resume. Remember that potential employers will be looking for three things:

☞ Skills and knowledge (horse or nonhorse) as they relate to the particular job
☞ The business, communication, and people skills you have that will contribute to a business's smooth operation and marketing
☞ Work habits and attitudes.

The first thing to put down on your list is your formal schooling—where you attended school, what diplomas or degrees you earned (or will earn soon), any academic honors you achieved such as American Legion Scholar or Dean's List, etc. Include any extra-curricular activities, too. Maybe you worked for the school paper as a reporter or were the co-captain of the basketball team or captain of your intercollegiate horse show team for two years.

If you were in the Boy Scouts of America for seven years and earned Eagle rank, add that to your brag list even though it may seem to have nothing to do with horses. If you studied trumpet for eight years and played with your school band, include that, too. Maybe you have been an active member of your church's youth organization and helped with food drives or other projects.

Put down any summer or weekend jobs and how long you held them. Include any unpaid volunteer work with equine professionals or veterinarians to gain experience. List your duties and how they may have changed over the time you were employed. If you worked the past four summers for a local landscaper mowing lawns and trimming trees, put that on your list; and if you moved up to supervising a crew of three people last summer, that surely goes on the list. If you worked weekends at a hack stable for the past year and moved up from grooming and saddling horses to leading rides, put it on the list.

Your list should obviously include all of your horse-related activities, what your level of involvement was, and how much personal responsibility you had for horse care, schooling, or any other phase of horse management. Maybe you never competed much but you trail rode regularly to keep your horse conditioned and helped your local trails association as part of a trail maintenance.

Were you ever responsible for caring for a friend's animals?

Every experience you have had working with horses is valuable and should be included on your resume.

Did you help coach younger members of the Pony Club you belong to? Maybe you were the secretary or treasurer of your 4-H club or helped organize one of the club's horse shows. What things have you done that demonstrated you can be responsible, persuasive, or trustworthy and work independently or solve problems? Make the list as complete as possible. Ask parents, friends, teachers, and club advisors to help you add to the list.

It is easy to sit down and make lists of your educational achievements and horse experience. It is much harder to show potential employers that you can take responsibility, follow through on assignments, and be persistent even when the tasks at hand may not be exciting. Look at your brag list and think about the character traits and skills that your activities represent. Shuffle the list and see what things appear as your strongest traits. Use the objective eye of a parent or school advisor to help you shuffle your list and organize your accomplishments according to what each one says about the skills, character, or work traits you possess. You will use the list of skills to write your resume, the work traits when you write a cover letter.

THE RESUME

Brag list in hand and reorganized, you are ready to paint a more formal picture of yourself for employers—a resume. A resume is your basic tool for approaching any potential employer.

A RESUME SHOULD INCLUDE:
- ✓ Your name, address, and phone number at the top of the page
- ✓ Either a two- or three-sentence summary of your background as it relates to your job goal *or* a one-line statement of what your job goal is
- ✓ Your previous job experience
- ✓ Your skills
- ✓ Your education
- ✓ Other significant accomplishments such as licenses or certificates you hold; any special activities or awards that could be relevant to the position you want.

There are two ways you can organize this information: **in reverse chronological order** *or* **by functions or skills**. Which way is best depends on both your own background and the job you are applying for.

When most people think of a resume, the reverse chronological resume is what most commonly comes to mind. It lists your work experience starting with the most recent position you have held and working back to earlier jobs. This kind of resume is best for people who have a steady job history. For each position you held, you indicate how long you held that job and what your duties and responsibilities were. If your job experience is scanty or you have skipped around among many different types of jobs or jobs that are not related to your current job objective, a reverse chronological resume may not give a potential employer an accurate picture of what you have to offer.

A functional, or skills resume organizes both your paid and unpaid experience according to the skills you have acquired. This kind of organization works best when you have worked for only one employer, or when unpaid horse care, club work, and school courses are your primary sources of skills and experience. Now your brag list comes into play. It might show that you have acquired skills in *horse care* (maybe your own horse, horses of friends on vacation, or your college's school string); *equitation* (lessons throughout high school and college, a B-level rating with your local Pony Club, show awards including one year-end high-point trophy); *instruction* (teaching younger Pony Club members plus experience as an assistant instructor during a one-semester internship arranged by your college); or *business management* (you were Pony Club treasurer for three years, assisted with the travel arrangements for your intercollegiate riding team as a junior, and maintained the health records of the college's school string as a senior project).

The functional resume allows you to think about how a job that at first appears totally unrelated to your horse goals might really relate after all. Take our example of someone who worked for a landscaping firm. That person acquired *mechanical* skills (working with mowers, trimmers, power saws, and other equipment) and *supervisory* skills (being in charge of a crew one summer). Both of those skills may be very useful to a potential horse industry employer, too. The applicant for a job as a veterinary technician who has previously held a job as a dental assistant has demonstrated an ability to work well in a supporting role for a doctor. A functional resume gives you a chance to organize those skills and present them to potential employers. With a computer to help juggle paragraphs, you can even customize each resume so you highlight the skills that are closest to each employer's needs.

How do all those extra-curricular activities fit into a functional resume? Some may have developed skills you could use in your future horse industry career. The person who wrote and reported for the school paper for several years has writing, editing, and perhaps even photography skills to list when applying for a position with an equine publisher. Our trumpeter and Eagle Scout may list *those* activities under "other accomplishments." Although they do not relate directly to horses, they do show that the job candidate has a sense of commitment, can work as part of a team, and can persist to reach a goal. Those may be just the traits the potential employer finds attractive in people he or she hires. The employer may also be impressed that the job candidate shows a well-rounded social life that has not been entirely horse-centered. That candidate may be better able to empathize with the employer's working clients and their efforts to juggle riding time, family life, and their own careers.

Most job-hunting experts advise against listing references in a resume. Instead, they say, only indicate on the resume that they are available. If you plan to use someone as a reference, you should ask them in advance. If they feel uncomfortable in that role, they have the opportunity to decline before a potential employer calls and puts them on the spot. You want your references to respond enthusiastically if they are called. Letters of reference from people in the horse industry who know you well can be useful marketing tools to carry to a job interview and leave with the interviewer. They must refer, however, to skills and character traits that would be of interest to your potential employer. If you ask someone to write a letter of reference, explain to them what kind of jobs you are applying for so they can keep that in mind as they write their letter. Ask if they would be willing to talk directly with potential employers about you.

Many books about how to write good resumes are available at your public library or through your school's guidance office. Getting outside help to make sure your resume is as strong as possible is a good idea. Your school's placement services may be able to help with resume writing, or check the Yellow Pages of your local phone directory for resume writing services.

Once your resume is written, ask one or more people to help you proofread it for errors in spelling or grammar. The resume is your potential employer's first impression of you. If it contains careless or sloppy mistakes, that first impression will be a poor one. Use a good electric typewriter or a letter-quality computer printer to produce a clean, crisp copy of the corrected resume, which can be reproduced in quantity by a copy shop.

continued on page 99

Marketing Yourself with a Good Resume

Jane is graduating from Horse Heaven University this spring and hopes to find a job as a lab technician or an assistant manager on a large breeding farm. The sample resumes and cover letter on the next few pages are part of a set of job-seeking tools Jane prepared as she approached graduation. Note how she incorporated both paid and non-paid jobs so that she could tell potential employers about *all* of her pertinent horse experience.

Before deciding on a course of studies at Horse Heaven University, Jane talked to a veterinarian whom she had accompanied on rounds for experience and to the farm managers of two large breeding farms she had located through ads in Thoroughbred and Quarter horse publications.

Throughout college, Jane worked to defray her expenses, and she made the most of that time by seeking out part-time positions that would enhance the job skills she would need in her intended career. ■

SAMPLE CHRONOLOGICAL RESUME

JANE RYDER
321 East Street
Piedmont, ND 65432
(901-234-5678)

Organized, detail-oriented horsewoman with 12 years of progressively more responsible horse-care experience. Familiar with veterinary and laboratory procedures for natural and artificial breeding. Business skills in record-keeping, customer relations, and inventory control.

EXPERIENCE

1993–PRESENT Laboratory assistant, Horse Heaven Stallion Station, Middleville, TN
* Assist with all laboratory procedures related to stallion station's breeding program including sperm counts, motility checks, and chilling, extending, and freezing semen
* Record keeping responsibilities include stallion medical records, shipping paperwork and stallion reports
* Assist veterinarians and farm manager with both natural breeding and artificial insemination

1991–1993 Assistant sales manager, Smalley's Tack Emporium, Middleville, TN
* Assisted customers in selecting appropriate merchandise
* Wrote bi-monthly customer newsletter with educational tips on horse care to complement store's monthly sales promotions
* Worked with distributor to develop automatic re-ordering system for grooming products, tack care products, and nutritional supplements

1988–1991 Farm caretaker, Gone Again Farm, Piedmont, ND
* In charge of feeding, stall cleaning, and turnout for six to eight horses including broodmares, foals, and yearlings at Quarter horse facility when owner away at shows

1988–1991 Piedmont Equine Clinic, Piedmont, ND
* Assisted Dr. Ned Dearing on weekend farm calls, attending to foaling broodmares, emergency first aid, and preparation of billing paperwork; received increasingly more responsible duties up to and including assisting with surgery

EDUCATION
Bachelor of Science, Veterinary Technology, with minors in Equine Studies and Business, Spring 1995, Horse Heaven University, W. Middleville, TN

REFERENCES
Available on request

SAMPLE FUNCTIONAL RESUME

JANE RYDER
321 East St.
Piedmont, ND 65432
(901-234-5678)

OBJECTIVE

Assistant manager/lab technician on large breeding farm

EXPERIENCE

HORSE CARE
* Assisting with both natural breedings and artificial insemination at university teaching facility standing eight breeding stallions
* Temporary responsibility for complete care of stable of up to eight horses including broodmares, foals, and yearlings while owner campaigned on show circuit for two seasons
* Stable manager at numerous U.S. Pony Club rallies, including the 1991 national rally, while earning B-1 rating with the Piedmont Ponytails Pony Club
* Care of personal riding horse for more than twelve years

LABORATORY
* Assisting with all laboratory procedures related to breeding program at university stallion station including sperm counts, motility checks, and chilling, extending, and freezing semen for transport
* Fecal egg counts and laboratory maintenance for large equine practice

BUSINESS
* Handling all shipping paperwork for transported semen from two stallions during the 1995 breeding season
* Assisting in meticulous maintenance of breeding records for eight stallions and proper filing of same with six breed associations
* Helping to develop automatic re-ordering system for high-turnover tack shop inventory
* Writing direct mail newsletter to support monthly in-store promotions

WORK HISTORY

1993–PRESENT	Horse Heaven Stallion Station, Middleville, TN
1991–1993	Smalley's Tack Emporium, Middleville, TN
1988–1991	Gone Again Farm, Piedmont, ND
1988–1991	Piedmont Equine Clinic, Piedmont, ND

EDUCATION

Bachelor of Science, Veterinary Technology, with minors in Equine Studies and Business, Spring 1995, Horse Heaven University, W. Middleville, TN

REFERENCES

Available on request

THE COVER LETTER

When you mail your resume to potential employers, it should be accompanied by a cover letter that includes:
- ✓ What position you are applying for
- ✓ How you learned about the position
- ✓ Why you are applying to that company or farm
- ✓ The character traits you have that could benefit the company or farm
- ✓ A request for an interview.

How you learned about the job may seem obvious—the employer placed a classified advertisement, filed a job offering with an employment agency, or contacted your campus placement office indicating a need. But if you heard about the job opening from a friend or former employer, mentioning this person's recommendation as the reason for your letter may help make a helpful personal connection with the person who receives your letter.

The reasons you give for **why you want the job** should include a few phrases or sentences to indicate you have done some homework about the company or farm and understand what makes them unique in their marketplace ("I am familiar with Leather Love's new leather care products targeted at horse show trainers and am intrigued by your unusual marketing approach.").

A statement about **how you can help the company or farm** with its mission should link your skills to the company or farm's needs. It should echo the information in your resume but not repeat it ("My responsibility for the Silver Saddles Ranch show tack for the past two seasons has given me an appreciation for the competitive edge that quality products provide.").

Your cover letter should end with a **positive statement** that you feel your skills could help the company with its mission, a **request for an interview**, and a brief **thank you** for the recipient's time. Your request for an interview should suggest a time ("I will be available for an interview in two weeks, after my final exams.") or should at least include an indication that you will call for a response ("I will call you at the beginning of next week to arrange a convenient time to meet you."). This is a good place to put the phone number where you can be reached. Even though it is on your resume, putting it in the cover letter, too, close to the end of the letter, makes it easy for the employer to respond.

Each cover letter should be customized to fit the situation of

SAMPLE COVER LETTER

321 East Street
Piedmont, ND 65432
Telephone: 123-456-7890
May 5, 1995

Mr. John Jockey
Plentifoal Farm
3 Raceway Drive
Lexington, KY 60606

Dear Mr. Jockey:

I am responding to your recent ad in <u>The Blood Horse</u> for an assistant broodmare manager at Plentifoal Farm.

I have long been aware of Plentifoal Farm's reputation for top-quality mare care and its state-of-the art on-farm lab. For the past two years, I have worked on the staff of Horse Heaven University's stallion station in Piedmont, North Dakota, where I have learned a great deal about the day-to-day management of breeding farms. My responsibilities for both laboratory work and breeding records increased significantly during this time. Several of my suggestions were incorporated into new forms adopted by the university last fall.

As I approach graduation in a few weeks, I am keenly interested in continuing to work in the breeding industry. The enclosed resume details my skill and work experience. I would welcome an opportunity to meet you in person to discuss how my combination of lab training, horse care experience, and business experience can make me a valuable member of your farm's staff.

Thank you for your consideration. I look forward to hearing from you.

Sincerely,

Jane Ryder

the employer you are approaching. Keep copies of each one and be sure to follow up with calls to those who do not call you. Studies show that only about 2 percent of the cover letters and resumes mailed out by job seekers result in interviews. When the job seekers make follow up calls, however, 20 percent of their mailings result in interviews.

THE BUSINESS CARD

One important marketing tool you should have is a business card. A business card does not need to have fancy graphics, give a "company name" or even list an occupation. Keep it simple. Printing just your name, address, and phone number in a simple, crisp typeface is fine. The idea is to have this important little marketing tool to leave with anyone you see during your job search. The person may not hear about a job tomorrow, but if they hear about one next week they will have your phone number handy to call you. Send a card with each resume. Keep a supply of your cards in your pocket at all times and hand them out liberally, always mentioning that you are looking for a position as you run through a personal, fifteen-second "commercial" (see page 103).

Putting your career package together is going to require an outlay of funds that you will have to budget for. Consider using a professional resume service, getting your resume printed by a quality copy shop, and printing business cards as an investment in your future.

Some malls now have self-service machines that print small quantities of simple business cards for a few dollars. That is one way you can keep your costs down. If you have access to a good laser or dot-matrix printer, you might consider printing your own business cards with a computer using some of the specialty card stocks available from mail-order stationary companies like Paper Direct (205 Chubb Ave., Lyndhurst, NJ 07071; 800-272-7377) or Paper Design Warehouse (1720 Oak St., Lakewood, NJ 08701; 800-836-5400). Don't be dazzled by all the colorful paper options in these catalogs—stick with a conservative plain vanilla paper for your job search. You can laser print ten business cards on each micro-perfed sheet, then separate the cards for distribution. For less than half the cost of getting 500 business cards printed by a regular print shop, you can print business cards in smaller quantities as you need them.

FINDING JOB LEADS

Job leads can come from a variety of sources:
- ☞ Your school's placement office
- ☞ Family, friends, and acquaintances in the horse industry
- ☞ Classified ads
- ☞ Employment agencies
- ☞ Targeted resume mailings.

School placement offices should be the starting point in your job search. Their job is to provide guidance for your search process. Make use of any services they offer to help with resume or interview preparation even if they cannot offer specific job leads that mesh with your career goal. If you attend a large university, there may be someone in the school of agriculture or its animal science department who fields job requests related to equine businesses.

Some equine studies programs make extravagant claims about placement rates in their recruiting literature. If you followed the advice in Chapter 2 and checked out the reality of these claims before packing your bags, you should not run into disappointment at this stage in your career pursuit. A few schools do have such good reputations that horsemen regularly seek out their graduates. However, the jobs available at any given time can fluctuate greatly depending on the economy, a temporary trend in the horse industry, or just luck. The school that placed half of its students in their first job choice and another 25 percent in their second choice last year may struggle to find job offers for 25 percent of *any* of its people next year.

Networking is the best way to locate the most jobs. According to the U.S. Department of Labor, almost two-thirds of all job seekers find a position through personal contacts, either by talking directly with employers or networking with people in contact with those employers. Put another way, the more people you know, the more likely it is you will find a job.

If people do not know that you are looking for a job, they will not think to tell you if they know of openings nor will they think to recommend you. Let as many horse industry people as possible know that you are looking. Sit down and make a list of all the people your know who might either have job openings from time to time or know other people who do. This list should include your parents' horsey friends, people you have become acquainted with through showing or club work, people you have met at horse conferences or conventions, current or former riding instructors, clinicians you have worked with, your high school 4-H or youth group leader, your farrier, your vet, the tack shop you buy from, and anyone else who comes to mind.

Divide this list into people you know well enough to approach in person and people you know less closely who should be approached by sending a resume and cover letter. Make it a point to contact a certain number of these people each week as you approach graduation.

Before you approach your "in person" list, prepare a short, concise "commercial" to explain to them what kind of job you are looking for and why you would be a great person to hire: "When I graduate from Horse Heaven College in June with a degree in Agricultural Communications I would like to find a position in marketing with a breed association. Our Block and Bridle Club annual horse show drew a record-breaking crowd the year I did publicity. I really enjoy promotion." Practice your little promotional speech until you know it cold then repeat it to anyone who will listen. It should take no more than fifteen or twenty seconds.

Horse shows are ideal for "networking." You never know who your future employers may be—and they might be watching you!

Each time you make a contact in person, leave a business card with your name and address and offer to send a resume. Be sure you get their address and phone number if they answer in the affirmative, and be *sure* you follow up and send that resume. Ask each person you talk to if they can suggest anyone else you might contact. Get two other names every time you talk to someone and you will be able to fling your net even wider.

Some of your contacts may be potential employers. In this case, treat any face-to-face contact as though it is a kind of mini-interview because it just may become that. Watch your personal appearance and manners just as carefully as if you had prepared for a real interview.

Set up a "tickle file," a system to keep track of your contacts and the results. For each person, keep records of who recommended that you contact them, what farm or company they work for, their phone number and address, the date you contacted them, what happened when you contacted them, and any follow-up calls or other actions you need to take.

Another way to make direct contact with potential employers is to write, sending a resume and cover letter that requests an interview. Besides talking to your school placement office and asking friends and acquaintances for likely names, you may locate good leads in horse publications that serve the segment of the horse industry where you hope to find a career. If you want to work in a specific geographic region, see if anyone has compiled a horsemen's directory specifically for that region and analyze its listings for potential employers. The career descriptions in Chapter 7 list directories that may be useful for specific careers.

A FEW DIRECTORIES updated annually that can provide leads for a broad range of careers are:

• ***Horse Industry Directory*** (American Horse Council, 1700 K Street N.W., Washington, D.C. 20006-3805; 202-296-4031; $20 or free to members) is the bible of the horse industry. It lists the addresses, phone numbers, and persons to contact for horse breed associations, sport or show associations, racing organizations, race tracks, equine publications including regional directories, rodeo organizations, trail organizations, transportation companies and much more. If you can't find the information you need in this publication, a little diligent research using the names that are here will lead you to what you want. Believe me, it's in there.

• ***Tack 'N Togs Annual Buyer's Guide*** (Miller Publishing, P.O. Box 2400, 12400 Whitewater Drive #160, Minnetonka, MN 55343; 612-931-0211; $25) is a directory of manufacturers of every kind of horse merchandise available plus their suppliers and distributors. There are names, addresses, phone and fax numbers for everyone producing equine goods from A to Z. This is an extremely useful directory for anyone contemplating a career in manufacturing, sales, or marketing.

• ***The Source*** (The Blood Horse, 1736 Alexandria Drive, P.O. Box 4038, Lexington, KY 40544-4038; 606-278-2361; $19.95 plus $2.00 postage and handling) is a comprehensive listing of people and services in the North American racing and breeding industry including the predictable lists of trainers and race tracks but also many professionals such as architects, auctioneers, landscapers, lawyers, financial consultants, painting contractors, and insurance companies who work with horsemen. There are lots of potential employers here you won't find in other directories.

• **U.S. Animal Health Directory** (Brakke & Associates, 2925 LBJ Freeway #153, Dallas, TX 75234; 214-243-4033; $200.00) is a book worth searching for if you are interested in a career in veterinary pharmaceuticals—either manufacturing them or marketing them. Again, you get names, addresses, phone and fax numbers for key contacts.

• **AFIA Membership Directory** (American Feed Industry Association, 1501 Wilson Blvd., Arlington, VA 22209; 703-524-0810; $100.00) is another book worth finding if this industry is your career goal. It lists the names, addresses, and phone numbers of people in sales, product development, and other areas of feed manufacturing throughout the U.S.

If your school placement office does not have copies of these directories or of the more specialized ones listed in Chapter 7, see if they would be willing to buy them for student use. Your department might convince the university library that some of them would be useful reference books, or you might ask the library to try to locate them through an interlibrary loan. Local vets and other professionals may have copies of directories they would be willing to let you use if you call and make an appointment.

Classified ads are another way to find job leads. With over 250 publications serving many small niches in the horse industry, it is easy to find equine publications that target segments of the horse industry where you would like to work. Your school may subscribe to some of them, you can ask among friends and acquaintances to see who might subscribe to others, or you can call the publications directly (find the phone numbers in the *Horse Industry Directory* listed above) to find out how to purchase the most recent issue or two.

Employment agencies offer one more avenue for job leads. Three within the horse industry that actively pursue jobs leads and job candidates, each with a slightly different approach, are:

• **Equimax®** (Equimax U.S.A., Inc., HC 65, Box 271, Alpine, TX 79630; 800-759-9494 or 915-371-2610) is a continuously updated classified advertising list in two parts—one listing jobs and the other listing job candidates. For $45, job candidates can advertise their availability in an open listing for any of ten geographic regions and also receive the list of current jobs; confidential listings are $70. Employers can list jobs and subscribe to the list of candidates. Employers can also purchase the list of candidates and contact likely persons directly without listing any job openings.

• **Professional Equine Employment** (P.O. Box 5, Spring Grove, VA 23881; 804-866-8975) works with its employer/clients to develop accurate job descriptions and a firm idea of the character traits the employer expects of the people working for him. Job seekers fill out detailed applications that describe their education, experience, and goals. Then Professional Equine Employment acts as matchmaker, recommending suitable applicants to the employer. If the applicant is offered and takes a job, applicant and employer share in the cost of the employment agency's fee, which varies depending on the type of listing.

• **Temporary Horse Care** (P.O. Box 711, Versailles, KY 40383; 606-873-9618 or P.O. Box 4781, Ocala, FL 34478; 904-622-2040) screens and places temporary employees primarily in the Thoroughbred industry; after 6 weeks, if the employee and employer agree, the employee can transfer to permanent status.

Until you find a job, search for opportunities to increase the number of contacts you have with people in the horse industry so you can put the word out that you are interested in finding work. Some activities, like showing, can put you in contact with a great number of potential employers over a very short period of time. Attending shows, meetings, conventions, auction sales, and other large gatherings gives you the opportunity to discuss your future plans with a great many people who may know employers looking for help. Keep your pockets full of those business cards.

THE INTERVIEW

Eventually your persistence will pay off with a request from a potential employer to come and meet face-to-face. When you go to the interview, put a fresh copy of your resume and business card with your letters of reference in a pocket folder to hand to your interviewer. If appropriate, you may want to include other pertinent items. If you are applying for a job as an instructor, you might include a copy of a student evaluation sheet you developed for use with lesson programs. If you are applying to a farm that conditions sales yearlings, you might include a quality photocopy of a "trophy photo" of the winning halter colt you conditioned as a project for an equine course. Our Horse Heaven graduate might want to include a copy of the program from her Block & Bridle show. An aspiring equine journalist applying to a horse industry publication could include one or two clips of her published writing from the school paper or a club newsletter.

One or two items pertinent to the position you are applying for can be ice breakers that move the interview to your strong points. But don't clutter your presentation folder with too many things. Your folder becomes something you can leave behind to remind your interviewer of the things you discussed.

First impressions count. Dress neatly and appropriately for the position you are interviewing for. Be prompt and remember that a firm handshake and eye contact are important as you meet your interviewer. Be natural and let your interviewer talk and lead the conversation. When the interview ends, politely suggest a time when you might call again to see if a decision has been made. Then be sure to get that date into your tickle file and follow up with the call.

If the answer is no, thank the interviewer for his or her time, and ask if the person knows of any other contacts in the field that might be useful. Try, again, to get two more names and phone numbers to continue your search.

If the answer is yes, be sure you are clear about the salary being offered; whether you will be paid weekly, bi-weekly, or monthly; what the job's hours will be; and what vacation, medical care, dental care, retirement, or other benefits are included. Then get ready for your first day on the new job!

CAREER CLOSE-UP

INSURANCE AGENT

Debi DeTurk remembers herself as a typical teenage girl in love with horses. "I was convinced that I was going to set the world on fire as a trainer and rider and it was all going to work out," she recalls. The reality of two severe injuries smashed her dreams of glory in the show ring, but today she stands on the other side of the rail, rubbing elbows with A-circuit owners, trainers, and riders as a personality in her own right.

Debi has become a highly respected equine insurance agent.

As a teen, Debi mucked stalls seven days a week to afford a horse. In high school, she enrolled in a work-study program so that she could finish her studies by late morning, then head to the barn for the afternoon. After her first injury, her father insisted that she at least apply to one or two colleges as a backup plan, even though she was determined to become a professional rider after finishing high school. Just months before she finished high school, she reinjured herself and was told she would never ride again. "Had I not been forced into applying for college," she admits with hindsight, "I would have been up the creek."

Debi earned a degree in journalism, then took a job in computer sales. She learned how to make sales presentations and build a client base. Still, she kept up with the horse world. One day she read an ad in a horse publication from a company looking for people with sales experience who also loved horses. Debi threw her resume into the pot. Out of 300 people who applied for the job, Debi was the only one with sales experience. She clinched the job.

Like many sales people, Debi works out of her home and car rather than settling down in an office each day. A typical day may start with the buzzing of her fax machine at 8:30 a.m. and can build to a brisk pace if a client needs an underwriting decision quickly before close of business. Debi might drive to a local destination to discuss a policy with a client, do some research on the value to place on a horse,

line up building inspectors to evaluate a facility whose owners want fire insurance, or call a veterinarian for a professional opinion on a horse's soundness. A lot of time is spent making sure paperwork is filled out correctly and processed in a timely manner.

Debi's sales territory is defined by the hunter-jumper disciplines she serves. That often means a lot of time on the road as she follows the show circuit wherever the horses and people go. Debi notes that initially, her salary with the insurance company represented a 25 percent cut in pay from her previous job. However, her sales commissions grew as she developed a client base. "I was told it would be three years before I was profitable to the company, and that was right," she says. Her gamble paid off, however. "Down the road, I think sales is the one area where you actually have a chance to make some money," she says. Looking back, she is delighted with her career evolution and delighted that she has found a way to combine her passion for horses with her profession. ∎

Chapter 6

Starting a Business

Many equine occupations are really small one-person businesses. If you decide to be your own boss working as a farrier, an equine artist or photographer, or a freelance riding instructor or trainer, the success of your business will depend not only on your career-related skills but also on your business skills. If you become a retail tack shop owner, a horse show manager, or a veterinarian with your own practice, or decide to produce and sell your own special-recipe horse treats, your business savvy will become even more critical as you learn to manage personnel, suppliers, and inventories.

Many long-time horsemen struggle to make a living despite having excellent horse skills. They live from day-to-day on the cash flow from yesterday's receipts because they have never mastered basic principles that should guide any business. They never turn enough profit to put money in the bank. Any windfalls that come their way are used to pay catch up—buy the replacement equipment they have been putting off, repair the truck, or paint the barn which should have been painted two years ago. They never get ahead.

Being in business for yourself does not have to be that way. The key, again, is *planning*. It is impossible to go into great detail about every aspect of starting and running your own business in a single chapter. What we can do is highlight the important steps any start-up business should go through and suggest some other sources where you can find more detailed information.

Business is a big word that covers a vast array of situations. At one end you have farriers working alone with a truck as an office, freelance riding instructors or trainers with minimal overhead, and people running small stables with fewer than a dozen boarders. Somewhere in the middle are slightly more complex businesses, such as a veterinarian with one partner and four employees working out of leased office space; a show barn with thirty horses, fifty clients, fifteen employees, and a big mortgage; or a manufacturer turning out a single product for the equine market from her own small warehouse with five to ten employees. Still higher in complexity, would be large stallion stations or broodmare operations with thirty to forty employees and a large investment in land; or manufacturers with multiple products, overseas sales, sixty or seventy employees, and millions of dollars in annual sales.

Chapter 5 described how to approach the businesses at the middle and upper levels we just described when you are looking for an employer. The businesses at the first level are the ones you run yourself, creating your own job. You and you alone control your destiny. You, and you alone, are also completely responsible for your income, health and dental benefits, vacation time, retirement savings, and any other perks an employer might provide for employees. Before you start out on your own, you need to figure out if your proposed business can support you and then develop a plan that will ensure business success.

Like the job seeker in the last chapter who started a "tickle" file to keep track of contacts, you should start some files to help plan and launch your new business. Label these: MARKET RESEARCH, MARKETING, INCOME AND COSTS, BOOKKEEPING, and LEGAL. You may add others or subdivide each of these files as you go along, but these will get you started. A well-documented business plan is essential if you plan to approach relatives, friends, or a bank for funding to get the business up and running.

The field of equine sports massage is thriving—and most practitioners are self-employed.

SURVEYING THE MARKET

Market research is the first step in planning your business. In Chapter 2, you looked at the amount of income you needed for living expenses, savings, and taxes. Market research involves taking a look at your proposed business to see if there will be enough customers for your product or service.

To decide if there are enough customers, you must decide just what business you will be in. That may seem ridiculously simple at first. "I want to be a farrier" or "I'm going to be a riding instructor" sounds pretty clear. However, within those categories, there are market niches, and it is impossible for one person to be good at all of them.

For example, our farrier might decide that his business will focus on pleasure horses, draft horses, five-gaited show horses, Thoroughbred racehorses, reining horses, show hunters and jumpers, etc. He might shoe a few horses in several segments of the horse industry, but his initial decision about the market niche he plans to target will affect his geographic base, the size of the territory he must cover to do business, the amount he will be able to charge for his services, even the kind of inventory he will have to stock.

Besides the logical break between Western and English styles of riding, our instructor may decide to focus on dressage, jumping, reining, equitation, or some other individual riding discipline. She may decide to work primarily with children or with adults, with beginners or with more advanced riders, and she will probably draw her clients from a limited geographic area.

A horse photographer might decide to concentrate on hunter-jumper shows, a saddler may decide to specialize in trophy saddles, or a tack shop may cater to English riders, Western riders, or carriage drivers. Describe and define your market in as much detail as possible.

Now you need to do some market research to figure out if there are enough customers within that market to support your business. Given the parameters of geography, disciplines, demographics, or other ways you have defined your target market, you need to assess the number of **potential customers** out there:

❏ How many total horses or people are there who your product or service might appeal to?

❏ What percent of those horses or people might actually use your service?

❏ Do people seem to be buying more, less, or about the same amount of this service or product as they did several years ago?

❏ What factors might change their desire or demand for this service in the next few years?

Now take a look at people offering **competitive services**:

❏ How many other people are offering similar services or products?

❏ How much do they charge?

❏ Does your competition appear to have more work than they can handle or too little to keep them busy?

❏ What motivators can you offer in terms of pricing, quality, convenience, or other factors that might persuade their customers to buy that service or product from you instead?

One indicator of whether or not there is enough work to support more people in a service field is whether the people working in that field gain all their income from a single business activity or whether they find it necessary to combine income from several part-time services to make a full-time living. For example, if most of the equine photographers in a particular market are also shooting weddings and soccer teams to keep their bank accounts from failing, you could surmise that becoming an equine photographer in the same market might not provide you with a living wage unless you come up with a uniquely profitable way of doing business. Even veterinarians now act as product sales representatives for some kinds of non-proprietary merchandise in the health field to add to the bottom line of their small businesses.

Where do you find information about your potential customers? By being creative with the many available sources of information available to you. Breed associations, sport associations, horse magazines, regional or local horse organizations, extension service county agents, agricultural economists at land-grant institutions, and state horse specialists can provide you with a wide range of demographic information about horses and horse owners. National and regional directories can help you target both potential customers and competition.

For example, by comparing the United States Dressage Federations' directory of members to its list of instructors, you will be able to get a rough idea of the ratio of instructors to potential customers in a particular state and in what parts of the state dressage

ELEMENTS IN A BUSINESS PLAN

A business plan tells you what direction your business is headed in and outlines what route you intend to take to get there. It can also be used to check your progress periodically as you move toward goals. Below are some suggested elements of a plan for someone intending to open a stable where he or she would train horses and riders for the show ring.

SCOPE AND PURPOSE OF THE BUSINESS
    Type of horses to be trained and sold
    Type and level of riders who would be clients
    Number of horses to be trained each year
    Number of riders who would receive training

PREMISE ON WHICH THE BUSINESS IS FOUNDED
    Demand for training in this field
    Growth trends for this sport or breed
    Concentration of horses and riders in the area

MARKETING PLAN
    Advertising
    Farm image-building
    Client entertaining
    Showing activity

FARM PERSONNEL NEEDS
    Amount of your own personal labor
    Farm manager
    Assistant trainer or instructor
    Stable help
    Veterinarian
    Accountant
    Lawyer
    Management consultant

INCOME PROJECTIONS
    Sales of horses
    Sale of surplus land
    Show earnings
    Training fees
    Lesson fees
    Boarding
    Income from shows held at the farm
    On-premises tack shop
    Vending machines

EXPENSE PROJECTIONS
    Debt service
    Farm and vehicle maintenance
    Payroll
    Insurance
    Advertising
    Travel and entertainment
    Show fees
    Bedding
    Feed and supplements
    Veterinary care
    Farrier care
    Utilities
    Tack
    Stable supplies

APPENDICES
    Comparable horse sales prices
    Comparable real estate prices
    Survey of training and lesson fees in the area
    Synopsis of your expertise in the horse
      business
    Credentials of your advisors

riders seem to be concentrated. A reining-horse trainer might use National Reining Horse Association statistics to see which areas of the country show the most growth in riders and competitions.

If you plan to start a boarding facility, regional directories can give you an idea of how many facilities already exist in that geographic area and what services they offer compared to the ones you plan for your business. Horse magazines constantly gather demographic information about their readers to convince businesses that it will be worthwhile to advertise with them. Ask the ad representatives at regional horse magazines you plan to advertise in for their readership surveys. These can help you gauge both the number of potential customers and how to price your services to them.

Think about what useful local information might be available from town governments, Chambers of Commerce, and state agencies. If you plan to start a riding program that targets beginning riders with a thought to running a special summer day camp for Girl Scouts, what trend does the local school board predict for school-age populations over the next five to ten years? How many scout troops does the regional Girl Scout Council report within easy driving distance of your proposed base, and how many youngsters received horsemanship badges in the last few years?

The questions and the sources of information will be different for every business. An aspiring freelance equine journalist should ask how many horse publications there are, how many people are already writing for them, what their pay rates are, and how many magazines pay outside writers versus taking only free editorial material? Contacting the publications listed in the *Horse Industry Directory* (see Chapter 5) and asking for their writer's guidelines and pay rates would produce much of that market data.

You can get some of your best market information by networking with local horsemen to find out if there seems to be an unmet demand for the service you plan to offer. Ask at local tack shops about typical rates for lessons, board, or other services in the area. Check classified ads in regional horse publications.

Look anywhere you can for data and information on trends. For example, the information you gleaned from the American Association of Equine Practitioners directories at your vet school's library indicate that the number of equine veterinarians in the three-county area where you planned to set up a practice has gone from three to five in the last five years, while the state horse population figures you got from the state extension horse specialist have remained about the same or even dropped slightly. Data from the most recent American Veterinary Medical Association marketing study indicates that horse owners are not spending any more on health care per horse now than they did four years ago. Your market research may lead you to decide to look for another area to set up practice, figure out a specialty that will distinguish your practice from that of the other five practitioners already there, plan to work over a larger geographic area, or alter your plans in some other way.

While it is not technically unethical, calling a potential competitor for information on markets or how to break into their line of business is not likely to produce truly useful information. But calling someone working in your chosen field in a different geographic area or in a peripheral occupation may elicit useful information. For example, you may have studied demographic information from the American Cutting Horse Association and learned that many ACHA members are doctors, lawyers, and business owners. You would like to be a cutting horse trainer in Colorado. Cutting horse professionals in Georgia or New England may be willing to discuss how they target their markets with you.

The discussion of long-term trends in the horse industry in Chapter 1 can be a start to your market research but you need to customize it to your potential business. Simple common sense will tell you that someone who wants to shoe racehorses in Iowa or offer sleigh rides in Florida is going to have a tough go. But what about the person who is thinking of starting a boarding stable in an area that is rapidly suburbanizing? Will the ready access to customers outweigh higher property taxes and the potentially greater expense of meeting zoning and environmental regulations in a more densely populated setting than might be true twenty or forty miles farther out?

INCOME AND COST PROJECTIONS

As you have done your market research, you have started to identify the **prices** your potential customers are willing to pay for services or products like yours. A number of factors come into play here:

- ☞ The income of the potential customers
- ☞ The uniqueness of your product or service
- ☞ The amount and quality of the competition.

Competition can drive prices down only so far until either income, quality, or both begin to suffer. The relationship between price and quality is a classic one in business.

There are many occupations in the horse industry that, by their seasonal or sporadic nature, are almost never full-time jobs. Being a horse show judge, a ring steward, or an equine appraiser are prime examples. Each of these jobs might be a part-time sideline along with a full-time career as a trainer, instructor, or farm manager, but planning to earn a living doing one of these activities alone is not realistic. If you think you might be the exception to that rule, do a business plan and prove it to yourself one way or the other.

Many people in the horse industry try to make a full-time living by combining income from several part-time occupations. For example, take a woman who works as a free-lance riding instructor but also runs a tack exchange service out of the back of her van and dabbles in horse photography at local shows. We discussed this in Chapter 2 as a competitive factor that tends to drive income down in horse industry jobs. Trying to create a full-time income by combining two or more part-time jobs not only depresses the income of those trying to work full-time at a single occupation, it seldom works over the long haul.

Look at our instructor/tack retailer/photographer. She is trying to market herself in three different areas with completely different customer bases. She is juggling so many skills that she probably does not have a clear business identity among the potential customers in any of her three distinctly different markets. Giving equal attention to promoting all three services becomes increasingly difficult. She would find it impossible to give a fifteen- or twenty-second description of her work. Imagine for a moment a farm trying to raise and market Arabians, Quarter horses, and warmbloods at the same time for use in reining, driving, and dressage and you may see the dilemma more clearly.

If our instructor/retailer/photographer were to do a simple business plan for each of her activities, she would probably see that there are one or two areas where she has the potential to earn the most income. If she concentrates her efforts there and lets other activities go, her bottom line may actually improve.

There are times when several different business activities can complement one another. Our riding instructor may also take an occasional horse for training, buy and sell two or three horses a year, and write articles for a regional publication as a way to publicize her riding business. She should keep firmly fixed in her mind, however, which activity is her primary income earner so that it always takes priority over the peripheral activities that can drain away her time, energy, and focus.

The next step in your business plan is to figure out how much **cash you need to get started**. This involves sitting down and listing everything you will need to open your door for business or to offer your service—from the first business cards you print to the last lead rope and bucket snap.

Start with all the supplies your business will require. Those costs will obviously be very different for a veterinarian, a farrier, a horse photographer, and someone setting up a lesson stable. Ask others to help you with your list to make sure you haven't missed anything.

A basic list for a new business office will include a telephone, answering machine, stationery (including envelopes, business cards, even pre-printed invoices or contract forms), a computer and some business software, and miscellaneous supplies from pencils and pens to stamps and postal scales. A fax machine is optional but rapidly becoming a necessity for many businesses.

A photographer will need camera bodies, lenses, flashes, filters, tripods, camera bags, film, batteries, model releases, a light box, file cabinets with hanging file folders or some other filing system for negatives and prints, a computer with labeling software, labels, photographic marking pens, a magnifying loupe, picture folders, picture albums, and mailing envelopes and cartons.

The list for every service will be unique. Someone thinking of starting a boarding or training facility needs to add the costs of renting stalls in an existing barn or the cost of a loan to buy his or her own facility as well as the costs of horses, tack, stable supplies, and farm personnel. But these lists should give you an idea of how to go about making a list for your own service. Products will have many other start-up costs related to production.

Depending on the complexity of your business, there are two other costs you should add to your list of start-up costs:

✓ Advice from an accountant on how to set up your books, develop a monthly cash flow projection, pay taxes you are liable for in a timely manner, and handle the bookkeeping for employee-related matters such as Federal withholding, Social Security, and state Workers Compensation.

✓ Advice from a lawyer on the legal form your business should take, insurance needs, and any standard contracts (for boarding, leasing, horse sales, liability release, etc.) that may be useful in your business.

If you seek professional advice, ask among fellow horsemen or check regional horse directories to find the names of accountants and lawyers familiar with equine businesses and their peculiarities. Interview each professional before deciding whom to hire. Most professionals are willing to spend a brief amount of time with potential clients to discuss the client's needs, the services they can provide, and their fees. Choose someone who is willing to discuss fees up front, understands that you want to keep your start-up costs as reasonable as possible, is accessible and empathetic to your business goals, and whose personality is compatible with your own. A few hundred dollars spent organizing your business properly right from the start may save you from thousands of dollars worth of grief somewhere down the road.

These are the costs you will incur just to open your door or produce the first unit of your product. To stay in business, you will have additional, **operating costs**. For our photographer, that will include more film, batteries, expenses to run and maintain a car, food and lodging while away at overnight shows, lab expenses, mailing expenses, and, eventually, costs for camera repair or replacement. Our stable operator will need to tote up feed, bedding, wormer, veterinary expenses, shoeing, tack repairs, and the costs to maintain the farm's cars, trucks, tractors, and trailers.

Accountants break these costs down into fixed and variable. For example, a farrier's costs for his telephone, answering machine, truck, and tools are his fixed costs for shoeing. The actual pair of shoes he used on an individual horse, the nails, pads, bottled gas for his forge, and the gasoline to get to the barn are variable costs attributable to that individual horse.

PRICING YOUR PRODUCT OR SERVICE

In Chapter 2, we looked at the level of income you would consider comfortable. If you are being hired by someone else, it is a simple matter to compare any salary offered against your desired income level when you are applying for jobs

When you are considering being your *own* employer, you must add your own salary and benefits to all of the start-up and operating costs we just outlined. Every sale you make of a service or product must pay the operating costs attributable for that sale plus a certain amount of your start-up costs, plus a certain amount towards your salary. This means that a certain amount for start-up costs, a certain amount for operating costs, and a certain amount for salary have to be built into each sale. There are a number of formulas you can use and here is where an accountant can be of help in your business planning.

There is no such thing as a guaranteed income from your own business. Building a business takes time. While you are building your client base, you will have to live off savings (experts recommend a financial cushion equal to two or three times that "comfortable income" figure you came up with) since your business will bring in little in its first six months and may take three years to actually support you. Diligently keeping expenses as low as possible in those early months and years is essential to helping your new business build a good cash flow.

Let's take the example of our farrier again. Let's say he has start-up costs of $30,000 for a heavy-duty truck, tools, the initial inventory of shoes, a telephone and answering machine, a computer and some business software to help him run the business, a little advice from an accountant and a lawyer, his business stationery and cards, and some advertising to let people know he is in business. He decides he wants to pay off these start-up costs over a period of three years, financing the bulk of it through a loan on the truck. So he needs to earn $10,000 his first year to pay back his start-up costs; then he'll start saving money toward a new truck.

Now he needs to figure out what his operating costs will be. Talking with other farriers or working with his instructors at the farrier school he attended, he calculates how many horses he thinks he can shoe per week and how many weeks out of the year he will be shoeing and projects the number of horses he thinks he can shoe in a year. Let's say our hypothetical shoer knows that he will lose some shoeing time during the haying season, a lot of people in his area pull shoes for the winter, and he'd like to take some vacation time to take a pack trip. So he estimates he will shoe 1,500 horses this year.

Again getting help from seasoned farriers and suppliers, he estimates that his operating costs for shoes, nails, pads, hoof dressing, oakum, borium rods, gas and coal for his stove, and other supplies will be $8,000. He figures he will drive 16,000 miles in the course of doing business for a year, figures his gas

The farrier's skills and the tools of her trade are her most valuable business assets.

and maintenance costs at $ .32 per mile, and adds in the interest on his truck loan for a total truck operating cost of about $6,900. He estimates that his business telephone will cost him $100 monthly and that stationery, invoices, envelopes, stamps, and other office expenses will run another $100 monthly. He plans to spend about $1,000 for a regular directory ad in two regional horse publications. Medical insurance will claim about $4,000 in premiums.

Let's also say that this year our farrier would like to make a salary of $30,000, and let's not forget he is going to have to pay taxes. We'll figure he'll need to set aside about $6,000 for federal and state taxes plus Social Security (FICA) taxes.

Toting a third of his start-up costs plus his annual operating costs, we find out that our farrier has to gross $68,300 in order to earn his salary of $30,000 by the end of the year. If he shoes 1500 horses, he must charge an average of about $45.53 per horse to meet his income goal. As he prices his services for everything from a simple foot trim to a full set of custom forged shoes, he will need to keep this average in mind.

There are other ways a service business can work out its pricing. In our previous example, we figured how many times a year our farrier could perform his services and determined a charge per service. Another way is to figure what hourly rate you should be charging for your services. Like our farrier, an equine writer might charge a set amount for a routine press release or writing service. Many major projects may be billed on an estimated or actual hourly rate, however. Like our farrier, the writer would have to determine all of her costs of doing business, have a salary target in mind and figure out how many hours she has available to write for clients in a given year. The latter figure must be considered carefully because not all of the writer's business hours will be spent on activities she can charge someone else for directly. Hours spent marketing her services, managing the office, or mastering a new word-processing program, for example, must be indirectly charged to clients because they, too, are operating costs.

Let's say that our writer's total operating expenses for the year are $20,000 and she wants to pay off her start-up costs of $6,000 over three years. Like our farrier, she wants to make $30,000 and needs to put aside about $6,000 to pay her taxes. She plans to take two weeks of vacation and figures that out of every forty-hour week, she will spend twenty-five hours on projects that can be billed directly to clients. She needs to charge about $46 per hour to meet her income goal.

As a very rough idea of how your pricing must be structured to meet your income goals, small business gurus advise that you use a multiplier of between two and two-and-a-half times net income when figuring out what level of gross income (your sales before you deduct any expenses and costs) will produce a particular level of net profit (your salary and money available to reinvest in the business). In other words, if you want to make a $30,000 income after taxes, you need to earn $60,000 to $75,000 in gross revenue to achieve it.

LEGAL MATTERS

Our examples have assumed single people operating their businesses as sole proprietorships, which is the simplest form of doing business. It means that, as owner of the business, you owe taxes on the net profits coming to you as business income, even if you decide to reinvest some of the profits in a new truck, computer, or other equipment to keep the business running. As a sole proprietor, you are also personally responsible for the business and can lose any assets including your house, truck, horse, etc., if a court judgement goes against you in a lawsuit.

There are other **ways to organize a business**, each with its own separate tax and liability implications. Put *extremely* simply:

ORGANIZATION	WHO PAYS BUSINESS TAXES	WHO'S LIABLE
Sole Proprietorship	business owner	you as owner
Partnership	business (then each partner pays personal income taxes on his or her share of the money received from the partnership)	partners
"C" Corporation	corporation	corporation
"S" Corporation	business owner	corporation
Limited Liability Company	business owner	company

If your business becomes more complicated than just you and your truck or computer, you should discuss with a lawyer the pros and cons of all the different forms of business organization feasible for you. You need to be aware of all the legal and tax ramifications of how you structure and operate the business. Local Small Business Administration offices may be able to help you find a lawyer sympathetic to the needs of start-up businesses to keep expenses as low as possible.

Besides offering advice about the form your business should take and how to deal with liability exposures the business may have, a lawyer can also help you set up standard contracts that can result in fewer misunderstandings with customers and a better chance of collecting unpaid bills.

Depending on your business, some useful standard **contracts** might include:

✓ Liability release for recreational riders or students
✓ Liability release for horses you transport commercially
✓ Training agreement
✓ Boarding agreement
✓ Breeding agreement.

Before you start your business as a sole proprietor or any other form of business, you need to check with local officials about laws that will apply to your business. Zoning regulations are your first concern, but you also need to research any health, environmental, or other community regulations that might apply to your business, especially if you will be keeping horses. Know the provisions of your state's equine liability law, if any, to take full advantage of its protection.

Depending on your business, there may be state permits or licenses you must obtain, including a business identification number to collect any state taxes that apply to your product or service. Veterinarians, veterinary technicians, massage therapists, Thoroughbred trainers, riding instructors in Massachusetts, commercial horse haulers, and others need to obtain the necessary licenses they need before opening for business. At a minimum, you may be required to register your business under a unique "doing business as" name.

ACCOUNTING

To keep track of your revenue and expenses, you need to establish a good set of books and an efficient billing system. Cash flow can give the illusion of making money; and many horsemen simply use the checkbook as an accounting system, figuring that as long as there is money in the bank, they are OK. The problem with this simple cash flow system, however, comes when an unexpected expense runs the balance dangerously low or seasonal boom-bust cycles make it difficult to budget income over the entire year. It is important to keep your finances in order. Otherwise, you may end up like one stable manager who used up her inheritance before she found out she was losing money.

An accountant can help you set up a budget and monthly cash flow projection in a simple set of books that will keep you on track. He or she can also advise you on how to make timely payments for any taxes, including state sales taxes you may have to collect from your customers; how to set up an efficient invoicing and billing system; and how to IRS-proof your records.

For the computer literate, there are many good software programs that can help you set up accounts and get bills out regularly so that cash keeps flowing. Two popular ones useful for small sole proprietorships are *Quickbooks* (Intuit, 2650 E. Elvira, Suite

100, Tucson, AZ 85706; 415-322-0573) and *M.Y.O.B.* (Best!Ware, 300 Round Hill Dr., Rockaway, NJ 07866; 201-586-2200). These programs can help you keep your start-up costs low.

FINDING CUSTOMERS

An important part of running any business is marketing to bring in new clients. **Advertising and marketing** expenses should be included with your list of regular operating expenses when you make your business plan. Among the things that fall under marketing are:

- ☞ Your business stationery and business card
- ☞ Brochures
- ☞ Your business image including your personal appearance and that of your truck, your farm, your horses, your students—anything that reflects your attitude and level of professionalism
- ☞ Maintaining a mailing list of customers
- ☞ Direct mailings to reach current and potential customers
- ☞ Advertising in media that reach the customer base you identified in your business plan
- ☞ Other publicity including speaking to clubs, giving clinics, writing press releases, etc.

Like our job seeker in Chapter 5, you should develop a short, concise "commercial" describing your service or product that you can deliver in fifteen to twenty seconds whenever you meet a potential customer:

I shoe racehorses at tracks in New York and the Mid-Atlantic states. Right now I'm based at Belmont Park, where I'm shoeing for the track's three top trainers this season.

I specialize in shoeing that balances Paso horses to enhance their gaits. I'm based in California and do regularly scheduled clinics in Texas and Florida every year.

My clients are people who keep their horses at home. I meet them there for lessons, then the group comes together as a team at shows to groom and cheer for each other. We call ourselves the Saddle Bums.

I lease stalls at Underwood Farm where I teach dressage and jumping to beginning and intermediate riders using "fear-free" techniques I've developed especially for adult riders.

Maintaining a mailing list of existing and past clients can be one of the most important marketing steps a business takes. Computers are invaluable here because of the ability to code a database so that clients can be pulled up by various categories. Learn to use every opportunity to get the names of potential clients onto your mailing list—advertisements that invite a response, booths at trade shows or horse fairs, speeches to clubs, attendees at clinics, etc.

Regular advertising (note the key word is *regular*, not necessarily *splashy*) keeps your business's name in front of current and potential customers. The best mix of advertising for a particular business depends on a multitude of factors, but most marketing specialists recommend budgeting at least a small percentage of your annual gross revenue for advertising. *Equi-Marketing,* by Tracy Dowson (Pica Publishing, 3440 Youngfield St., Suite 354, Wheat Ridge, CO 80033) contains good advice on marketing and advertising geared especially to equine businesses.

FURTHER BUSINESS ADVICE

We have only scratched the surface of things you need to think about and do before hanging up your shingle or putting your business in the phone directory's Yellow Pages. Any public library will have many excellent business books explaining how to do market research, write a business plan, set up books, price your product or service, market your business, deal with customers, and supervise employees.

While you are still in school, see what business planning resources may be available to you through your college's business department. At a minimum, the business school dean's office may be able to recommend a senior or graduate student who would be willing to review and help you refine your business plan to ensure you meet your income goals.

If you are already out of school, check to see if the local high school or any nearby colleges offer adult continuing education programs in small-business management. Many do, and the instructors for these courses are potential sources of leads for bookkeepers, lawyers, and other consultants who can help you get your business started right. Government sources of free or almost free business information include:

- **U.S. Small Business Administration** (P.O. Box 15434, Fort Worth, TX 67119) offers more than 100 helpful booklets for a nominal fee on topics from finding financing to pricing, recordkeeping, budgeting your cash flow, preparing business plans, and marketing to help new businesses get organized. Local and regional Small Business Administration offices around the country offer free assistance to start-up and existing small businesses.
- **Service Corps of Retired Executives** (SCORE, 1825 Connecticut Ave. N.W. Suite 503, Washington, D.C. 20009; 202-205-6762) also provides free advice through business workshops and one-on-one relationships between entrepreneurs and an experienced mentor.
- **Internal Revenue Service** (Taxpayer Services, U.S. Department of the Treasury, 1111 Constitution Ave., N.W. Rm. 2422; Washington, D.C. 20224; 800-829-3676) offers several publications useful for small businesses including the *Tax Guide for Small Business—Publ. 334, Self-Employed Retirement Plans—Publ. 560,* and *Business Use or Your Home—Publ. 587.*

CAREER CLOSE-UP

FARRIER

Sizzle, smoke, and the scent of seared horn fill the aisle as Louise Clement fits a custom-forged shoe to the foot of her current client. She sets the horse's hoof down and carries the hot horseshoe, held firmly in farrier's tongs, back to her anvil for one final adjustment with a heavy, flat-faced hammer. The small forge mounted at the rear of her truck glows red as she reaches in with the tongs to retrieve another heated shoe.

Farriery is physical work. From lifting the 125-pound anvil in and out of her truck to hanging on when a 1200-pound horse decides to jerk its foot away while she is doubled over to tap a nail, Louise finds her fitness challenged every day. Horseshoeing challenges her mind, as well, and it is that aspect of her work that she finds so rewarding. "No foot, no horse" is an adage every horseman knows only too well. When an arthritic horse is able to move with a freer stride because of a change in its shoes, or a horse whose poor conformation predisposed it to interference moves a little straighter, Louise feels fulfilled. "I started shoeing to help horses," she explains.

Louise earned a degree in biology at Roanoke College in Salem, Virginia, and found a desk job in New York City after graduation. She quickly learned, however, that she hated the city and working indoors. She moved to California and found herself taking theory courses in farrier science at Santa Rosa Junior College. Hooked, she applied and was accepted at Danny Ward's horseshoeing school in Martinsville, Virginia. Few farrier schools accepted women in the late 1970s though that situation has changed considerably since then. After finishing Ward's program, Louise bought a used van and tools and returned to Westport, Connecticut—where she had grown up—to hang out her shingle.

To be a farrier, Louise observes, you must be organized and self-starting, the same traits any small-business person needs to be successful. There is no sick pay, medical insurance, vacation time, or disability pay unless you plan them

for yourself. You must be good at dealing with all kinds of clients, some pleasant and some unpleasant. Then there are the elements: A farrier contends with flies, heat, cold, wet, stomped toes, pricked fingers, rasped knuckles, and a perennial morning backache. Farriers put miles and miles on their vehicles every day as they drive from barn to barn. Louise also emphasizes that you must really like horses to put up with the punishment they can dole out.

It is that love of horses and the feeling that her work can help them that makes her job worthwhile, Louise says. "It's very rewarding to see a horse that was lame go sound, one that couldn't even walk take sound steps."

It is *that* satisfaction that keeps this farrier and her forge on the road. ■

Chapter 7

50 Careers in the Horse Industry

To help you with your career planning, here is specific information about 50 different careers within the horse industry. While these are only a fraction of the jobs available to horse lovers, they do represent a cross section of job types in the industry.

Working professionals were surveyed to obtain this job information. Although they in no way represent a statistical sampling of people working with horses, their comments offer a picture of what it is like to work for someone else, to be in business for yourself, to work directly with horses, or to work in one of the many jobs that means contact with horses on at least an occasional basis. Where associations have surveyed their professional members, their data was used to present as complete a profile as possible. Their information was compared with information gleaned from the classified ads in major horse publications, U.S. Department of Labor projections, and interviews with equine employment agencies.

A horse dentist examines his client.

Competition within a given geographic area can affect factors such as salary levels, the amount of experience or education necessary to qualify for a job, or the cost of starting a business. Grooms in Florida, New York, and California, for example, may all earn very different wages because the prevailing labor rates in each of those areas will vary to reflect different living costs. It is worth noting a theme running consistently through the survey returns. Although many reported that their jobs in the horse industry were not necessarily financially lucrative, they reported a very high level of job satisfaction: "I love this work!" "...very rewarding" "...tremendous creative flexibility" "It's a wonderful job...making my own hours and controlling my own destiny."

If you are interested in a specific career, use the contact sources suggested in each listing and in Chapter 4, Getting Experience, to find people working in these jobs in your area. Ask them to help you update the information here and relate it to your region and segment of the horse industry as you lay your career plans. Contact lists may also suggest potential employers and/or clients for people in particular professions.

ACCOUNTANT

Education Needed: Four-year degree in accounting

Certification: Certified Public Accountant examination required

Horse Experience: Not necessary but extremely helpful in understanding clients' businesses, especially if the accountant specializes in a particular market segment such as the racing industry

Job Description: Accountants help equine businesses set up their books, keep records, and pay taxes in a timely fashion. By specializing in different segments of the equine industry, accountants can become familiar with the cash-flow cycles and unique business rhythms of farms, tack shops, or service businesses. Few accountants work 100 percent in the horse industry. For most, equine businesses are only a percentage of the clients they serve. Accounting is a desk job with regular work hours and little horse contact. Some accountants join large firms and eventually work their way up to being partners, but many accountants are self-employed in this growing field. Their earnings are based on fees charged to individual clients. Once their practice is established, accountants tend to stay in the same place.

Potential Earnings: Entry level—$28,000; after ten years—

$50,000; top earnings—$100,000; start-up costs for a self-employed accountant—$25,000

Related Jobs: Lawyer, insurance salesman, bloodstock agent

Making Contacts: The national directories listed in Chapter 5 contain the names of accounting firms specifically working in the horse industry which can be approach for jobs as well as hundreds of potential clients for self-employed accountants. Use regional directories and regional horse publications to help build your equine contact list.

ANNOUNCER

Education Required: Four-year degree in communications

Certification: None

Horse Experience: Essential. Announcers generally become specialist-experts in a particular sport discipline and learn all they can about the horses and riders within it.

Job Description: Announcers provide informational patter for the entertainment of horse event spectators and provide coordination between event management and exhibitors to keep horse events running smoothly. They may work indoors in an air-conditioned, sound-proofed announcer's booth one day; the next weekend may find them nursing a cranky sound system under a hot, dusty tent. Most announcers are self-employed business owners who must hustle to market themselves since earnings are based on the number of shows they work and how much they can charge per show. Booking jobs often requires regional or national travel. They work very irregular hours with weekends being prime working days. Their contact with horses is primarily as observers rather than direct handlers. Announcers must stay cool under pressure, staying focused on classes while dealing with distractions, conflicting demands, piles of class lists, and hundreds of details. While event committees generally provide the sound system an announcer will use, announcers must be comfortable with all types of electronic equipment; the best ones can do a little trouble-shooting in a pinch. Those who enjoy a fast pace and variety find announcing an exciting job.

Potential Earnings: Entry level—$30,000; after ten years—$50,000; top earnings—$70,000; start-up costs—$2,000

Related Jobs: Horse show manager, television commentator

Making Contacts: Get lists of local, regional, and national shows in a particular sport discipline from individual sport associations or breed associations, and contact show management at least a year in advance of events where you would like to work; advertise in regional and national directories or publications dealing with your sport. American Horse Shows Association, 220 E. 42nd St., New York, NY 10017-5876; 212-972-2472. Professional Horseman's Association of America, 20 Blue Ridge Lane, Wilton, CT 06897-4127. United Professional Horseman's Association, 4059 Ironworks Pike, Lexington, KY 40511-8434; 606-231-5070.

APPRAISER

Education Needed: High school or more

Certification: Through American Society of Equine Appraisers, P.O. Box 186, 834 Falls Ave.–#1130, Twin Falls, ID 83303; 208-733-1122

Horse Experience: Extensive experience in breeding, sales, judging, training, or riding within a specific field (Thoroughbred race horses, hunters, reining horses, etc.) necessary to establish good credentials as an appraiser

Job Description: Appraisers help set a value on an individual horse for buyers, sellers, insurance companies, or auction companies. They must not only know how to evaluate a horse's conformation, temperament, athletic potential, or breeding potential; they must continually seek data on current market prices. Appraisers are usually self-employed and may travel locally, regionally, or nationally depending on their specialty. An appraiser spends approximately equal amounts of time looking at a horse then researching prices and writing up his evaluation. Appraising is primarily a part-time adjunct to a related equine occupation.

Potential Earnings: Appraisers usually work for a variable hourly wage (average: $60) that includes not only the horse evaluation but also their price research, write up, and travel expenses.

Related Jobs: Lawyer, bloodstock agent, insurance agent, auctioneer, judge, trainer, breeder, professional rider

Making Contacts: National and regional horse directories. American Society of Equine Appraisers, P.O. Box 186, 834 Falls Ave.–#1130, Twin Falls, ID 83303; 208-733-1122.

ARCHITECT

Education Needed: 5-year degree in architecture

Certification: By state architectural boards

Horse Experience: Important to fully understand the consequences of any designs

Job Description: Architects help horsemen design facilities for breeding, training, or exhibiting their animals. Depending on whether they are self-employed or work for someone else, all of the decisions about running and marketing the business may be their own, or their work may be directed and supervised by others. Self-employed architects earn money based on fees charged to each client rather than being paid a salary. Architects have little direct contact with horses, and their work may require regional or national travel although their work hours are predictably regular.

Potential Earnings: Entry level—$18,000; after ten years—$35,000; top earnings—no limit

Related Jobs: Construction, engineering, landscape architecture

Making Contacts: Architects listed in *The Source*, The Blood Horse, 1736 Alexandria Drive, P.O. Box 4038, Lexington, KY 40544-4038; 606-278-2361. Barn builders and stable suppliers in *Tack 'N Togs Annual Buyers Guide*, P.O. Box 2400, 12400 Whitewater Drive–Suite 160, Minnetonka, MN 55343; 612-931-0211. Construction firms advertising in regional and national horse publications.

ARTIST

Education: Highly variable from high school to specialized art school to bachelor's or master's degree in fine art. Some artists are self-taught, some advise finding a good mentor who can help the artist develop both creative and business skills.

Certification: None

Horse Experience: Knowledge of equine anatomy, animal motion, proper tack and attire for particular riding disciplines all essential

Job Description: Equine artists capture the spirit of horses on canvas or paper, in bronze or clay or other media. Some artists do specific portrait commissions; some create and sell prints or posters; others draw illustrations for books and magazines or become involved in design for posters, clothing, gifts, and greeting cards. Some do a little of all of these things in order to make a full-time living as an artist while many others pursue their career on a part-time basis. Artists estimate they spend about 25 percent of their time outdoors observing the horses they will draw, paint, or sculpt (an ability to use a camera well to photograph impressions for future reference can be very helpful) and 75 percent of their time indoors creating the work. Most artists are self-employed business owners whose work hours are highly variable and whose earnings are based on both fees for original works and sales of prints or designs. Commissions may find them traveling anywhere to observe their subjects. They enjoy almost full control of their time and the way they choose to work but must pay attention to marketing and deadlines. Many artists start out part-time with a very small investment and gradually build their professional reputation. Top fine artists are represented by galleries or other agents who help them sell their work for a commission.

Potential Earnings: Highly variable depending on whether they are working part-time or full-time; many artists work for little or nothing until their reputation becomes established. Entry level—$0 to $10,000; after ten years—$5,000 to $30,000; top earnings—$30,000 to unlimited for top artists with gallery representation; start-up costs—$200 to $2,000

Related Jobs: Commercial artist, gallery owner, photographer, clothing or gift design

Making Contacts: American Academy of Equine Art, P.O. Box 1315, Middleburg, VA 22117-1315. *Equine Images*, P.O. Box 916, 900 Central Ave.–#19, Fort Dodge, IA 50501; 800-247-2000 (magazine carrying advertising by equine artists seeking commissions).

ASSOCIATION MANAGER

Education: Bachelor's or master's degree in business, animal science, or management for management-level job; high school education or more for clerical personnel

Certification: None

Horse Experience: Preferable to be familiar with the breed or sport discipline but not essential as long as candidate is willing to learn

Job Description: Association executives and their staff people manage breed registries, distribute rule books, publish magazines and other equine literature, schedule and organize major events such as shows and trade fairs, lobby for horse interests before government bodies, promote their breed or sport, help equine professionals market their services, and perform many other business-related services within the horse industry. Equine associations range from very small breed registries run by volunteer staff to major breed and sport associations working internationally as well as nationally. Association managers report a high level of satisfaction with the varied duties of their positions but caution that there is very little direct horse contact, and although they technically work regular hours, their jobs demand a lot of travel and extra hours on weekends, even holidays, for which they do not receive extra pay. Association managers and staff are always salaried employees answerable to whatever board directs their breed or sport. Associations are located all over the country although there tend to be concentrations along the East Coast and in the Midwest.

Potential Earnings: Entry level—$20,000 to $45,000; after ten years—$40,000 to $75,000; top earnings—$50,000 to $120,000

Related Jobs: Financial manager, accountant, lobbyist

Making Contacts: American Society of Association Executives, 1575 Eye Street N.W., Washington, D.C. 20005; 202-626-2723. *Horse Industry Directory*, American Horse Council, 1700 K Street N.W.–Suite 300, Washington, D.C. 20006-3805; 202-296-4031.

AUCTIONEER, AUCTION SALES MANAGER

Education: High school, technical school, or bachelor's degree in business or marketing; on-the-job-experience most essential

Certification: None

Horse Experience: Experience helpful in appraising horses and goods; knowledge of buyers and industry essential for understanding how to structure a sale, advertise, and motivate buyers

Job Description: Auctioneers, auction managers, and their staff provide essential marketing services to horsemen. Auction sales provide a regular marketing channel for livestock and a pricing benchmark for those selling their animals or goods through other means. They must not only know how to organize and run sales but also keep current on marketing conditions throughout the country. Some auction sales personnel are employees of large auction houses; others are self-employed business owners whose earnings are based on fees for managing a sale and/or commissions on the amount an auction sale brings in. They spend from 10 to 40 percent of their time in direct contact with horses, and their time working indoors vs. outdoors breaks out at about 50/50. Hours are irregular and travel can be extensive.

Potential Earnings: Entry level—$10,000 to $30,000; after ten years—$20,000 to $40,000; top earnings—$25,000 to $75,000; start-up costs for self-employed—$25,000

Related Jobs: Appraiser, trade show manager, pedigree analyst, sales manager, accountant

Making Contacts: *The Source*, The Blood Horse, P.O. Box 4367, Lexington, KY 40544-4367. *Horse Industry Directory*, American Horse Council, 1700 K Street N.W.–Suite 300, Washington, D.C. 20006-3805; 202-296-4031.

BLANKET CLEANING SERVICE MANAGER

Education: High school, on-the-job training in sewing and repair

Certification: None

Horse Experience: None needed to perform the service but helpful in marketing it

Job Description: Blanket cleaners wash and repair horse clothing for those who lack the heavy-duty washing and sewing machines (or time) to perform these services themselves. They may also provide pick-up and delivery services as part of their marketing strategy. Blanket cleaners are self-employed business people who work primarily indoors with little or no direct horse contact and tend to work within a limited geographic area. Their earnings are based on the number of blankets they clean and how much they charge for cleaning or repairing each one. Blanket cleaning is a seasonal business with long hours required during spring and summer, less time during fall and winter. For that reason, some blanket cleaners consider their job a part-time/seasonal occupation; others look for work outside the horse industry to keep their machinery investment working full-time year-round.

Potential Earnings: Entry level—$10,000 to $20,000; top earnings—$35,000 to $60,000; start-up costs $20,000

Related Jobs: Tack shop repair service

Making Contacts: Find clients through local and regional horse publications, tack shops, and major stables in the area.

BLOODSTOCK AGENT

Education: Four-year degree in business or marketing

Certification: None

Horse Experience: Extensive knowledge of the Thoroughbred market essential for understanding market values, building a client base, and networking to find buyers

Job Description: Bloodstock agents work primarily in the Thoroughbred industry performing a multitude of related services for horse owners and breeders. They act as brokers for sales or purchases, do appraisals, prepare youngsters or older horses for auction sales, place insurance, arrange legal advice for partnerships and syndicates, do accounting, do pedigree research and analysis, design advertising and marketing programs, contract for horse transportation, and make breeding arrangements. In short, a full-service bloodstock agent holds a Thoroughbred owner's hand through nearly everything his or her horse does except training and racing. Full-service bloodstock agents must have a deep knowledge of not only Thoroughbred horses but also of human nature. Their work brings them in daily contact with horses. Work hours are long and irregular for these self-employed individuals with lots of weekend work and travel required, even internationally, as many agents represent their clients in overseas transactions. Earnings are based on a mix of flat fees for some services, such as appraisals or boarding for sales prep, and commissions of 5 percent for arranging sales and purchases. Commissions mean that lean and fat years can easily occur back-to-back. Some bloodstock agents specialize in only a few of the many services others provide, but as the Thoroughbred market shrinks, many agents find they must branch out into other services in order to make a living.

Potential Earnings: Entry level—$0 to $15,000; after ten years—$25,000 to $60,000; top earnings—$60,000 to $70,000; start-up costs depending on range of services—$8,000 to $100,000.

Related Jobs: Auction sales, training stable manager, breeding farm manager, insurance agent, lawyer, accountant, pedigree analyst

Making Contacts: *The Source*, The Blood Horse, P.O. Box 4367, Lexington, KY 40544-4367.

BOARDING STABLE OPERATOR

Education: High school plus business training; associate's or bachelor's degree in equine studies

Certification: None

Horse Experience: Extensive experience in stable management, horse health, horse behavior, and an ability to work well with all kinds of horses

Job Description: Boarding stable operators provide basic care for horses whose owners lack the time or facilities to care for their animals themselves. A boarding stable operator must be a jack-of-all trades and willing to tackle any job regardless of how menial to keep a facility humming. Knowledge of horses, machinery, and people are all essential. The operator must also be a sharp business person who keeps good books because the success or failure of a boarding operation depends in large part on his or her ability to keep expenses pared to the bone. Boarding operators carry heavy expenses for their mortgage or rental costs, utilities, employees, insurance, and machinery as well as obvious things like feed and bedding. Geographic location, special amenities for boarders or their horses, and extra services offered can all affect the bottom line significantly. They enjoy daily contact with horses working very long hours that continue through weekends and holidays. Many boarding stable operators augment their boarding income by hiring trainers or riding instructors who work at the facility for a commission on their lessons. Others are part-time operators boarding only one or two horses to defray the costs of their own horse.

Potential Earnings: Highly variable depending on the size of the facility, its geographic locations, etc. Aim for a certain profit per month per horse after accounting for *all* expenses; i.e., someone who wants to net $30,000 from a fifteen-stall facility must net at least $167 per stall per month. That amount, plus each stall's proportionate share of expenses, cannot exceed the going rate for board in your area. Start-up costs—$50,000 to $300,000 or more depending on the size of the facility and the cost of the land.

Related Jobs: Farm manager, trainer, riding instructor

Making Contacts: Local and regional horse publications. Local veterinarians, tack shops, feed dealers, and local riding clubs.

BOOKSELLER

Education: High school or more; business education very helpful

Certification: None

Horse Experience: Not necessary, but any horse experience helps in understanding the market and the factors that will be important to your buyers

Job Description: Horsemen are voracious readers and equine booksellers serve their appetite for knowledge. Some distribute only new horse books (and videos) produced by various

publishers. Others seek out and resell rare and out-of-print books in many fields. As self-employed business people, their earnings are based on the volume of books they sell, so they must be good at marketing and advertising to keep turning over their inventory. Bookselling primarily provides part-time income to those interested in limiting work hours or selling equine books as an adjunct to other kinds of book sales. Booksellers work almost entirely indoors with little or no direct contact with horses. There is a growing trend toward marketing books through booths at horse shows and trade events, which involves some travel.

Potential Earnings: Start-up—limited until established; after ten years—$10,000 to $15,000; top earnings—$20,000 to $25,000; start-up costs—$1000 and up for inventory and advertising

Related Jobs: Publisher, librarian

Making Contacts: American Booksellers Association, 282 S. Broadway, Tarrytown, NY 10591; 914-591-2665.

BROODMARE MANAGER

Education: Four-year degree in equine studies or animal science

Certification: None

Horse Experience: Basic knowledge of horses paramount, then on-the-job experience; must have an ability to work with horses of all types and temperaments

Job Description: Broodmare managers often start out on the bottom of the stable ladder mucking stalls, learn more as they go, and eventually work their way up. They must have good general knowledge of horses and stable management as well as specialized knowledge of the feeding, veterinary, and other special needs of broodmares. Good record keeping and office skills are essential, as thousands of dollars may be at stake when records are lost or mishandled. About 75 percent of their time is spent outdoors and in daily contact with horses, the other 25 is spent indoors and handling paperwork. Broodmare managers are generally salaried employees in charge of any-where from a few mares at a private farm up to several hun-dred at a large farm owned by multiple partners. As they take on more responsibilities, particularly at larger establishments, the best managers become eligible for commissions and bo-nuses that significantly affect top earnings.

Potential Earnings: Entry level—$18,000 to $20,000 sometimes with housing provided; after ten years—$30,000 to $40,000; top earnings—$100,000 or more

Related Jobs: Farm manager, head groom, breeding technician

Making Contacts: *The Source*, The Blood Horse, P.O. Box 4367, Lexington, KY 40544-4367. *Roster Of Corporations, Stables, and Farms*, U.S. Trotting Association, 750 Michigan Ave., Columbus, OH 43215-1191; 614-224-2291. Regional horse directories and publications, breed association membership lists, equine employment agencies.

CAMP DIRECTOR

Education: B.S. or M.S. in equine studies

Certification: American Riding Instructor Certification Program, P.O. Box 282, Alton Bay, NH 03810; 603-875-4000. CHA, The Association for Horsemanship Safety, 5318 Old Bullard Road, Tyler, TX 75703; 800-399-0138. Horsemanship Safety Association, Drawer 30, Fentress, TX 78622; 800-798-8106

Horse Experience: High level of competence as both rider and instructor essential in sport disciplines stressed by the camp; experience teaching youngsters and managing staff personnel very desirable

Job Description: Riding camp directors manage every facet of summer programs designed to provide an equestrian recreational experience for young people who may have little or no prior horse experience. Directing a riding camp is a very seasonable job but one that might well suit new graduates or full-time teachers looking for summer employment. They must have not only excellent teaching skills, but also excellent people skills so they can organize and direct the work of teaching assistants, stable help, and the campers themselves. Directors are responsible for the health and well-being of a string of horses being used fairly intensively, so a high degree of general horse knowledge is essential. Camp directors work straight through the camping season with only occasional days off. They may work six days a week or have two or three days off between camping sessions and are required to be available at the camp location at all times while under contract for the season.

Potential Earnings: $150 to $400 per week

Related Jobs: Riding instructor, groom

Making Contacts: American Camping Association, Bradford Woods, Martinsville, IN 46151-7902; 317-342-8456. Associations listed above, equine employment agencies, regional horse publications.

CHIROPRACTOR

Education: Veterinary school or chiropractic school with additional training in animal chiropracty

Certification: American Veterinary Chiropractic Association, P.O. Box 249, Port Byron, IL 61275; 309-523-3995. State board exams

Horse Experience: Knowledge of horse anatomy and an ability to work well with all types of horses essential

Job Description: Equine chiropractors make small adjustments in a horse's spinal column in order to help him work to his athletic potential and minimize pain caused by misalignment of the vertebrae. Some equine chiropractors are state-licensed veterinarians, others are state-licensed chiropractic practitioners. Both doctors must take additional training in animal chiropractic techniques, pass a written examination and then subject case studies in order to earn certification as an animal chiropractor. Equine chiropractors work daily with horses and most travel out to where their patients are located. As self-employed business people, they must market their practice and supervise office staff as well as seeing horses.

Related Jobs: Veterinarian, veterinary acupuncturist, equine massage therapist

Making Contacts: American Veterinary Chiropractic Association (address above). American Chiropractic Association, 1701 Clarendon Blvd., Arlington, VA 22209; 703-276-8800.

CONSTRUCTION CONTRACTOR—BARNS AND ARENAS

Education: Four-year degree in agriculture, agricultural engineering or business

Certification: None

Horse Experience: Very desirable to be familiar with the needs of horses and horsemen; and the features that make barns easy or hard to work in, and safe or unsafe for horses

Job Description: General contractors and their crews erect barns, arenas, storage buildings and other farm structures for horseman. A general contractor must be able to plan, estimate, price materials, and supervise crews. Construction workers may specialize in carpentry, masonry, electrical work, excavating, or plumbing. Construction is primarily an outdoor job but

remodeling of older buildings can mean indoor work. General contractors are self-employed business people whose earnings come from a percentage of profit built into their estimates; if their estimates are off, their income will be, too. They need to plan on a few lean years at the beginning of their career while they become established. Construction workers earn hourly wages.

Potential Earnings: Entry level—$0 to $18,000; after ten years—$25,000 to 50,000; top earnings—$50,000 to $75,000

Related Jobs: Fencing contractor

Making Contacts: Lists of barn builders in *Tack 'N Togs Annual Buyers Guide*, P.O. Box 2400, 12400 Whitewater Drive–Suite 160, Minnetonka, MN 55343; 612-931-0211; and *The Source*, The Blood Horse, P.O. Box 4367, Lexington, KY 40544-43667. Local and regional horse publications.

DENTAL TECHNICIAN

Education: B.S. in animal science, equine studies or veterinary technology; on-the-job training

Certification: International Association of Equine Dental Technicians, P.O. Box 6095, Wilmington, DE 19804-6095; 800-334-6095

Horse Experience: Must be able to get along well with all types of horses

Job Description: Equine dental technicians use heavy files to smooth rough edges called "hooks" off of horses' teeth so they can carry a bit in their mouths comfortably and chew efficiently without bruising or cutting their tongue or cheeks. Those interested in becoming dental technicians usually learn by apprenticing to an established technician; otherwise, most dental technicians are self-employed business people. Equine dental technicians must be patient, possess considerable strength and physical stamina, and have a solid knowledge of the anatomy of the horse's skull. Some dental technicians work part-time, others full-time, but all travel extensively within a regional territory to work daily with their equine clients and some may work nationally. One day they may work in a climate-controlled barn, the next in an open field. They work with veterinarians when problems such as wolf teeth or impactions call for minor surgery. Most dental technicians have good working relations with veterinarians in their area. However, anyone planning to enter this field should be aware that the practice of equine dentistry by anyone other than a licensed veterinarian is technically illegal in almost every state. Veterinary associations vigorously oppose non-veterinarian dental technicians on the grounds that equine dentistry is a medical procedure and, in part, to defend an income source for their members. In practice, many veterinarians look the other way and ignore the activities of competent dental technicians working in their area because veterinary schools offer little practice in equine dentistry, they lack the physical size or strength required (especially on larger horses), they see removal of hooks as a management procedure more akin to farriery than to medical science, or they prefer spending their case time on medical procedures they find more rewarding to perform. This is currently a gray area that may become more black-and-white in the future.

Potential Earnings: Entry level—$25,000; after ten years—$40,000 to $60,000; top earnings—$70,000

Related Jobs: Veterinarian, veterinary technician

Making Contacts: International Association of Equine Dental Technicians (see address above). Local veterinarians and regional horse directories.

EVENT MANAGER

Education: Four-year degree in marketing, communications, public relations, business

Certification: None

Horse Experience: Beneficial to have a solid working knowledge of the horse industry and the needs of horsemen in order to communicate and plan well

Job Description: Horse show and trade show managers plan and put on events to attract horse exhibitors, attract the general public, or both. They must be able to do long-range planning involving the orchestration of thousands of details from stalls and shavings to exhibitor's passes and portable toilets. They must be skilled at working with people, finding good suppliers, and hiring reliable personnel to actually run the event. Today's economics also demand that event organizers be good at wooing sponsors to help defray costs. Event managers are generally self-employed business people although a few are salaried employees of associations. Their work is generally split between indoor office work and outdoor work at show grounds and the like, but there is little direct horse contact except during events. Managers may be hired by an organization for a set fee, paid a percentage of the gate, or a combination of the two.

Potential Earnings: Entry level—$20,000 to $30,000; after ten years—$35,000 to $50,000; top earnings $70,000 to $100,000

Related Jobs: Association management, manufacturer's sales representative

Making Contacts: Breed, sport, and show organizations listed in *Horse Industry Directory*, American Horse Council, 1700 K Street N.W.–Suite 300, Washington, D.C. 20006-3805; 202-296-4031.

EXERCISE RIDER

Education: Associate's or bachelor's degree in equine studies

Certification: None

Horse Experience: Excellent riding skills essential plus an ability to work with all types of horses, particularly young horses

Job Description: Exercise riders work at farms helping to train young horses or at tracks developing fitness in racing Thoroughbreds. While their duties may be limited to riding if they work at a track, exercise riders on Thoroughbred farms are also expected to care for horses, including weanlings and yearlings, and to pitch in on any stable management chores from aisle sweeping to foaling watches. Exercise riders need not be as lightweight as jockeys, but trainers and farm managers generally set 135 pounds as their upper weight limit. Although exercise riders enjoy lots of daily contact with horses, they often have little say in how or when they work with their charges. These are jobs for people who enjoy rising very early, working very hard, and take direction from others. Exercise riders earn a weekly salary and housing is often provided by farms. When an exercise rider regularly rides particular horses for a trainer, the trainer may offer a small percentage of any purses the horse wins as a bonus. Some exercise riders use their experience galloping horses and meeting trainers as a step toward becoming a jockey.

Potential Earnings: Entry level—$10,000 to $11,000 with housing; after ten years—$13,000 to $15,000 with housing; top earnings—$18,000 to $20,000

Related Jobs: Stable manager, broodmare manager, groom, assistant trainer

Making Contacts: *The Source*, The Blood Horse, P.O. Box 4367,

Lexington, KY 40544-43667. Equine employment agencies, classified ads in Thoroughbred publications. Horsemen's Benevolent and Protective Association, 2800 Grand Route St. John, New Orleans, LA 70119; 504-945-4500.

EXTENSION HORSE SPECIALIST

Education: B.S., M.S., or Ph.D. in equine studies, animal science, agriculture, or education

Certification: Civil service examination may be required

Horse Experience: Solid general knowledge of horses and a working knowledge of the horse industry essential, but expert riding skills or specialized knowledge not required

Job Description: Extension horse specialists in many states have an educational mission. Their job is to communicate the latest findings of researchers at major agricultural institutions, primarily land-grant colleges, to horsemen in practical, useful ways. They spend about 70 percent of their time indoors, have daily contact with horses from 20 to 80 percent of the time, and travel throughout their state meeting with horse groups and individual farm owners. Many manage their state's 4-H horse program and are often responsible for organizing horse events including shows or equine trade fairs. There are also extension agents working with 4-H clubs and individual horse owners at the county level, although their work never focuses entirely on horses.

Potential Earnings: Entry level—$20,000 to $22,000; after ten years—$30,000 to $40,000; top earnings—$50,000 to $70,000

Related Jobs: Teaching, research

Making Contacts: U.S. Department of Agriculture, Cooperative Extension Service, Washington, D.C. 20250 for list of states with horse extension specialists. *Horse Industry Directory,* American Horse Council, 1700 K Street N.W.–Suite 300, Washington, D.C. 20006-3805; 202-296-4031. Land-grant universities.

FARM MANAGER

Education: High school, plus vocational training, associate's or bachelor's degree in equine studies or animal science

Certification: None

Horse Experience: Essential in whatever phase of the horse industry the farm serves—breeding, boarding, racehorse lay ups, etc.

Job Description: Farm managers are responsible for keeping horse facilities running smoothly and in good repair. They need not only horse skills to keep their equine charges healthy and safe but also many other basic skills from carpentry to pasture management, tractor maintenance, supervision of farm personnel, and bookkeeping. Hours can be long and irregular, including frequent weekend work. Farm managers are salaried employees who are often given great autonomy. They often begin as stable help, learn on the job, and gradually take on more responsibility. Those who enjoy daily contact with horses and a primarily outdoor lifestyle find these jobs rewarding.

Potential Earnings: Entry level—$18,000 to $22,000; after ten years—$25,000 to $30,000; top earnings—$35,000 (all including housing)

Related Jobs: Head trainer, head groom, broodmare manager, farrier

Making Contacts: Equine employment agencies, classified ads in regional and national horse publications.

FARM SITTER

Education: High school or higher; some business training highly desirable

Certification: None

Horse Experience: Essential to be able to deal with all types of horses and a wide variety of caretaking situations

Job Description: Farm sitters take over horse care and farm management duties on a temporary basis when owners or managers need to be away from their farms. While owners are away at shows, on vacation, or sick themselves, farm sitters take over feeding, mucking, turnout, blanketing, administration of medications, and other daily horse chores for them. They may or may not perform other services for owners including feeding and caring for other pets, waiting for vets or farriers, or arranging for deliveries of feed or bedding. They must be available seven days a week, flexible about hours and working conditions, able to follow each owner's or manager's instructions precisely, and utterly dependable regardless of weather, sickness, transportation breakdowns or other calamities. Farm sitters may be part-time or full-time self-employed business people. They charge for their services by the day, the trip, per horse, or some combination of these factors and they may include mileage charges for longer trips. Their rates will vary widely from one area of the country to another depending on the cost of living there. The concentration of horses within a given geographic area and the number of horses per day the sitter can care for limit how much a farm sitter's business can grow. In areas with many horses, farm sitters may hire helpers to build their business.

Potential Earnings: Entry level—$0 to $10,000; after ten years— $15,000 to $20,000; top earnings—$20,000 to $25,000 for someone working full-time and hiring others in their business; start-up costs—$3,000 to $5,000

Related Jobs: Groom, assistant farm manager, humane investigator, assistant trainer

Making Contacts: Local or regional horseman's directories, local or regional horse publications. Area tack shops and veterinarian's offices. Good business organization advice: *The Professional Pet Sitter*, by Lori and Scott Mangold; Paws-itive Press; P.O. Box 97280-0911; 800-47408738; $29.95 postpaid.

FARRIER

Education: Farrier's school certificate, A.A. or B.S. in equine studies with specialty in farrier science; business courses extremely helpful

Certification: American Farrier's Association, 4059 Iron Works Pike, Lexington, KY 40511; 606-233-7411. Brotherhood of Working Farriers Association, 14013 East Hwy. 136, LaFayette, GA 30728; 706-397-8047

Horse Experience: An ability to work well with all types of horses essential

Job Description: Farriers trim feet and shoe horses to help them deal with the rigors of various kinds of footing and to correct as far as possible for foot abnormalities, unsoundness, or other problems that affect the equine gait. New farriers may apprentice with experienced working farriers for awhile after earning a farrier's certificate, but most farriers work independently as self-employed business people, and many work only part-time. Their work involves extensive travel, so the greater the concentration of horses, the easier it will be to earn a good living. Most farriers fashion mobile horseshoeing shops in the bed of a pickup truck and travel to shoe from six to ten head of horses daily. Some specialize in particular breeds or sport disciplines such as Thoroughbred racing. Horseshoeing is extremely physical, primarily outdoor work often performed under less-than-ideal conditions and with a high risk of personal injury. Farriers must be able to deal not only with horses but also with people, and they must have good business skills.

Potential Earnings: Entry level—$10,000 to $20,000; after ten years—$25,000 to $50,000; top earnings—$50,000 to $70,000; start-up costs for truck, portable forge, and other tools—$10,000 to $30,000

Related Jobs: Farm manager

Making Contacts: American Farrier's Association and Brotherhood of Working Farrier's Association (addresses above).

FEED DEALER

Education: High school plus vocational agriculture and business courses or four-year degree in agriculture, agri-business, or related fields

Certification: None

Horse Experience: Very helpful when working on problems of storage, handling, and acceptance of feeds by horses

Job Description: Feed dealers stock and sell retail feeds for all kinds of livestock including cattle, hogs, sheep, and poultry as well as horses. Most tend to affiliate with a particular feed company or a few non-competing companies with different lines. The trend is toward fewer and larger feed stores with many feed cooperatives also branching out into the pet food market. This means feed dealers must be knowledgeable about a variety of livestock species and ready to help their customers choose among options. Feed dealers must also master business skills including inventory control, personnel management, retail space management, and bookkeeping. Feed dealers work both indoors and outdoors and tend to work long hours that wrap around weekends. As business owners, their eventual salary depends on the overall profitability of their dealership.

Potential Earnings: Entry level—$15,000 to $18,000; after ten years—$25,000 to 30,000; top earnings—$30,000 to $50,000; start-up costs for buildings, delivery trucks and initial inventory—$100,000 to $300,000

Related Jobs: Retail tack shop owner, extension horse specialist

Making Contacts: American Feed Industry Association, 1501 Wilson Blvd.–#1100, Arlington, VA 22209-2403; 703-524-0810. Regional horse directories.

GROOM

Education: High school and on-the-job training, associate's or bachelor's degree in equine studies, animal science, or related field

Certification: None

Horse Experience: With employers seeking good grooms, extensive horse experience often counts more than education levels achieved.

Job Description: Grooms are responsible for the day-to-day care of horses on farms, in training or boarding stables, on the racetrack, and at competitions. They are often the glue that holds a good barn together because attentive caretaking can keep horses healthy and happy in their work. A good groom will catch small problems before they become big ones and take appropriate action. A groom's duties may include everything from mucking stalls, sweeping aisles, and raking stone paths, to monitoring medications, bandaging, cleaning tack, and managing turnout. Some grooms may be asked to function as occasional exercise riders, instructors, or assistant trainers as needs arise. Grooms are expected to be infinitely flexible, infinitely cheerful, able to take and follow orders, but also able to take initiative and think for themselves. It is no small wonder that many people lament good grooms are hard to find. Grooms work daily with horses, and their hours are irregular, long, and almost always include at least part of every weekend. In addition to weekly or monthly salaries, they often receive housing and sometimes other benefits such as lessons or riding privileges. Top grooms often go on to become managers at their own or other stables.

Potential Earnings: Entry level—$10,000 to $12,000; after ten years—$15,000 to $18,000; top earnings—$20,000 to $25,000 (all including housing)

Related Jobs: Assistant trainer, assistant riding instructor, breeding farm assistant, assistant farm manager, exercise rider

Making Contacts: Farm listings in *The Source*, The Blood Horse, P.O. Box 4367, Lexington, KY 40544-43667 or in directories for major sport disciplines (see appendix). Regional horse directories. Horseman's Benevolent and Protective Association, 2800 Grand Route St. John, New Orleans, LA 70119; 504-945-4500 (racing).

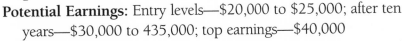

HUMANE INVESTIGATOR

Education: Four-year degree in equine studies, animal science, law enforcement plus in-service training in animal abuse

Certification: State certification required for animal control officers

Horse Experience: Essential in order to distinguish normal ranges of equine caretaking, training, and exhibiting situations from those that may be abusive

Job Description: Humane investigators may work as government animal control officers with legal authority to make arrests and seize property or as animal investigators for humane organizations that work as educators to reverse abusive situations and report intractable abuse cases to animal control authorities. Trained animal investigators may be called upon as expert witnesses in court cases. Knowledge of animals other than horses is essential as horses are a minor part of the national animal abuse picture. Humane investigators work both indoors and outdoors and their hours can be highly irregular. Many are unpaid volunteers, some are part-time salaried employees, others are full-time employees of humane associations or local governments.

Potential Earnings: Entry levels—$20,000 to $25,000; after ten years—$30,000 to 435,000; top earnings—$40,000

Related Jobs: Groom, humane association staffer, animal control program coordinator, animal rehabilitator

Making Contacts: In-service training in equine investigation available through American Humane Society, 63 Inverness Drive East, Englewood, CO 80112; 303-792-9900; and the Hooved Animal Humane Society, 10804 McConnell Rd., Woodstock, IL 60098-0400; 815-337-5563. Also contact National Animal Control Association, P.O. Box 1600, Indianola, WA 98342; 800-828-6474. Listings for equine welfare organizations in *Horse Industry Directory*, American Horse Council, 1700 K Street N.W.–Suite 300; Washington, D.C. 20006-3805; 202-296-4031.

INSURANCE SALES AGENT

Education: Associate's or bachelor's degree in business, animal science, or related fields

Certification: State licensing required to sell insurance

Horse Experience: Not absolutely required but extremely helpful in dealing with customers and their concerns

Job Description: Equine insurance agents help horse owners protect themselves from the financial blow of heavy medical costs or the loss of a particularly valuable horse. Farm insurance agents help farms protect themselves against losses from fires, natural disasters, lawsuits by disgruntled or injured persons, and other business catastrophes. Some insurance agents work regular hours primarily out of an office while others hustle on the road visiting farms, attending shows, and meeting people face-to-face to market the lines of insurance they represent. Their hours are far more irregular but their activity brings them in direct contact with horses more often. Insurance involves a great deal of paperwork that must be filled out correctly and handled in a timely fashion. Computer literacy is a must. Building a client base can take several years as one learns sales techniques and finds a market niche, so beginners are advised to have a cushion of savings to carry them through two or three lean early years.

Potential Earnings: Entry level—$0 to $20,000; after ten years— $30,000 to $60,000; top earnings—$100,000 or more

Related Jobs: Appraisers, underwriters, adjustors, accountants

Making Contacts: Membership directories of breed and sport associations listed in *Horse Industry Directory*, American Horse Council, 1700 K Street N.W.–Suite 300, Washington, D.C. 20006-3805; 202-296-4031. Regional and national horse publications.

LAB TECHNICIAN

Education: B.S., M.S., or Ph.D. in chemistry, genetics, or other biosciences

Certification: None

Horse Experience: Not essential

Job Description: Lab personnel range from those processing samples from horse shows, race tracks, and veterinary practices to researchers designing biological studies and laboratory directors supervising groups of technicians. Lab personnel are usually salaried employees who work regular hours and do little traveling. They seldom work directly with horses unless drawing blood or taking other tissue samples for research projects.

Potential Earnings: Entry level—$25,000; after ten years— $30,000 to $50,000; top earnings—$70,000

Related Jobs: Veterinarian, veterinary technician, researcher, racing chemist

Making Contacts: North American Veterinary Technician Association, P.O. Box 224, Battle Ground, IN 47920; 217-351-2418. Association of Official Racing Chemists, P.O. Box 19232, Portland, OR 97280; 503-644-9224. Laboratories listed in *The Source*, The Blood Horse, P.O. Box 4367, Lexington, KY 40544-43667. Research facilities at land-grant universities.

LAWYER

Education: Four-year degree plus doctor of jurisprudence degree

Certification: Must pass board exams to practice in individual states

Horse Experience: Not essential but helpful when dealing with equestrian clients

Job Description: Lawyers help equine business owners set up their operations to help minimize tax exposure and potential liability. They advise on the best way to structure the business, insurance needs, and standard contracts required. Those forming syndicates and partnerships in the racing industry turn to lawyers to help meet the concerns of all parties. Most lawyers who specialize in legal matters pertinent to the horse industry do not spend 100 percent of their time on equine law but must develop a mix of equine and other clients. Some 70 percent of lawyers are self-employed business owners, usually in some sort of partnership arrangement, rather than salaried employees of a firm. They need marketing skills as well as legal knowledge and an ability to work well with many different kinds of people.

Potential Earnings: Entry level—$0 to $24,000; after ten years—$25,000 to $100,000; top earnings—$150,000 or more; start-up costs—$10,000

Related Jobs: Accountant, tax preparer, paralegal

Making Contacts: Attorneys listed at county law libraries, or in *The Source*, The Blood Horse, P.O. Box 4367, Lexington, KY 40544-43667. Directories of sport associations listed in *Horse Industry Directory*, American Horse Council, 1700 K Street N.W.–Suite 300, Washington, D.C. 20006-3805; 202-296-4031. *Martindale Hubbell Law Directory*; 121 Chanlon Road, New Providence, NJ 07974; 908-464-6800.

LIBRARIAN, MUSEUM CURATOR

Education: M.S. in library science, museum studies, or art history

Certification: None

Horse Experience: Not essential but helpful to be able to communicate with horsemen and understand industry terminology

Job Description: Librarians and museum curators in the equine industry preserve data and history for current and future generations. Research libraries maintain information used by veterinarians, researchers, educators, journalists, and others. Other libraries and museums collect valuable books, papers, and artifacts on various facets of the equine industry for preservation, research, and display. Sport and breed organizations use museums as tools to reach and educate the general public. Librarians and museum curators are salaried employees who work very regular hours and often travel nationally in their work. They enjoy a relatively high degree of autonomy in deciding when and how to do their work.

Potential Earnings: Entry level $20,000 to $25,000; after ten years—$28,000 to $35,000; top earnings—$40,000

Related Jobs: Education, public relations

Making Contacts: Libraries and museums listed in *Horse Industry Directory*, American Horse Council, 1700 K Street N.W.–Suite 300, Washington, D.C. 20006-3805; 202-296-4031. American Association of Museums, 1225 Eye St., N.W.–Suite 200, Washington, D.C. 20005; 202-289-1818.

MANUFACTURER'S SALES REPRESENTATIVE

Education: High school plus sales experience or four-year degree in marketing, business, or a field such as equine studies, animal science, or agriculture relating to the products you plan to sell

Certification: None

Horse Experience: Many manufacturers require sales representatives to be active participants in horse sports that will bring them in contact with buyers and keep them aware of buyer preferences.

Job Description: Manufacturer's sales representatives are independent business owners who take sales orders from retail outlets, such as catalogs and tack shops, for one or more manufacturers or product lines. Sales representatives may come in direct contact with horses a certain percentage of the time especially if the products they represent require it (such as a saddle sales rep doing saddle fittings). They travel three to four days a week to meet directly with retailers and even large farms that may buy directly from them. Sales reps also represent their manufacturers and product lines at equine trade shows. These salesmen work on straight commissions, usually 10 percent of sales. As small businesses, sales representatives are responsible for their own business costs including phone, travel, insurance, Social Security, taxes, etc. Their earnings potential is limited only by the size of their territory, their personal energy, and their mastery of good sales techniques.

Potential Earnings: Entry level—$0 to $20,000; after ten years—$35,000 to $60,000; top earnings—$70,000 to $100,000 (all gross income figures)

Related Jobs: Retail tack shop owner, catalog seller, wholesale distributor

Making Contacts: *International Saddlery And Apparel Journal*, 1130 Guynn, Paint Lick, KY 40461; 606-986-3044. *Tack 'N Togs Annual Buyers Guide*, P.O. Box 2400, 12400 Whitewater Drive–Suite 160, Minnetonka, MN 55343; 612-931-0211. W-E Source, 1226 W. Bayaud, Suite 300, Lakewood, CO 80228; 303-914-3000.

MARKETING SPECIALIST

Education: Four-year degree in marketing, business, public relations, or journalism

Certification: None

Horse Experience: Not essential, but general knowledge of the horse industry and horse sports extremely helpful

Job Description: Marketing specialists work with associations, events, and manufacturers to promote their interests to the general public, potential sponsors, and the media. They make decisions about where to advertise, mount trade show exhibits, write proposals to solicit sponsorships, and develop media campaigns to draw spectators to events or new products to horsemen. Their work is highly variable but usually involves little direct contact with horses. Marketing people frequently travel around the country for their employers. About half of all equine marketing specialists are self-employed business people.

Potential Earnings: Entry level—$15,000 to $20,000; after ten years—$25,000 to $35,000; top earnings—$40,000 to $50,000; start-up costs—$10,000

Related Jobs: Advertising, public relations, journalism, sales
Making Contacts: *Horse Industry Directory*, American Horse
  Council, 1700 K Street N.W.–Suite 300, Washington, D.C.
  20006-3805; 202-296-4031.

MASSAGE THERAPIST

Education: Certificate from equine massage course, courses in
  equine anatomy
Certification: TT.E.A.M. Training International. International
  Equine Triggerpoint Myotherapist Association; others pending
Horse Experience: As much hands-on experience as possible and
  an ability to get along with all kinds of horses
Job Description: Massage therapists work horses' muscles to promote circulation, relieve soreness and tension, and increase
  body awareness. Their goal is to help the horse reach its fullest
  athletic potential. Equine massage therapy is such a new field
  that there is little standardization of techniques or training.
  Training sessions may last from a few days to almost three
  months. Techniques include TT.E.A.M. touching and body
  awareness training, acupressure, sports massage, trigger point
  myotherapy, percussion, cross-fiber massage, and others. Each
  has its ardent advocates. Concern among veterinarians about
  uniform qualifications will probably lead to a specified training
  program leading to national certification in the near future.
  Massage therapists are self-employed business people who
  travel widely to reach their clients. Their income will depend
  on motivation, energy, and mastery of marketing skills.
Potential Earnings: Entry level—$5,000 to $10,000; after ten
  years—$10,000 to $35,000; top earnings—$40,000 to
  $50,000; start-up costs—$5,000
Related Jobs: Equine chiropracty, equine veterinary acupuncture
Making Contacts: International Association of Equine Sports
  Massage Therapists, P.O. Box 447, Round Hill, VA 22141; 800-
  843-0224. International Equine Triggerpoint Myotherapist
  Association, 249 Mountain Rd., Granby, CT 06035; 203-653-
  9150. TT.E.A.M. Training International, P.O. Box 3793, Santa
  Fe, NM 87501-0793; 505-455-2945.

NUTRITIONIST

Education: Ph.D. in animal/equine nutrition, or D.V.M. plus post-
  graduate studies in equine nutrition
Certification: None

Horse Experience: Not essential but helpful to have general knowledge of horses and horse behavior

Job Description: Equine nutritionists strive to apply the latest in research findings to the rations modern horsemen feed their animals. They can be found teaching and doing research in universities, as employees of large feed companies, and as independent consultants working with individual farms and smaller feed companies. Their work brings them in direct contact with horses about 25 percent of the time as they travel nationally to meet with other researchers and with clients. They must be comfortable working with computers and computer models, have good people skills, and keep up with volumes of scientific literature to stay current in their field.

Potential Earnings: Entry level—$40,000; after ten years—$80,000; top earnings—$120,000; start-up costs—$5,000 to $8,000

Related Jobs: Feed dealer, feed sales representative, commodity buyer, drug company sales representative, feed additive sales representative

Making Contacts: Equine Nutrition and Physiology Society, 309 West Clark St., Champaign, IL 61820; 217-356-3182. American Feed Industry Association, 1501 Wilson Blvd.–#1100, Arlington, VA 22209-2403; 703-524-0810.

PHOTOGRAPHER

Education: Technical school, four-year degree in fine arts, or on-the-job experience

Certification: None

Horse Experience: Essential to know horse behavior, breed conformation standards, and performance standards required in different sport disciplines

Job Description: Horse photographers capture special moments or create special portraits for horse owners, publishers, advertisers, and others. They must have an intimate knowledge of equine behavior and how to influence it in order to set horses up properly for portraits and anticipate the peak of action at sporting events. Technical familiarity with their camera equipment is a given, and good equipment requires a substantial financial outlay in the beginning. With the exception of a few magazine staff photographers, equine photographers are self-employed business owners who must find and develop their special market niche to be successful. Some photographers specialize in conformation photography of specific breeds at farm locations; others follow the racing circuit; still more follow the show circuit for particular disciplines like dressage, hunter-jumpers, or cutting. Competition is fierce. Full-time professional photographers must compete with the many part-time photographers who lack the business skills to price their photographs profitably as well as with Uncle Joe, who takes his for free. Photographers trying to earn a full-time living from their craft usually shoot horses as only one of several markets they sell to.

Potential Earnings: Entry level—$0 to $5,000; after ten years— $18,000 to $25,000; top earnings—$40,000 to $50,000

Related Jobs: Advertising, publishing, videographer

Making Contacts: Publications listed in *Horse Industry Directory*, American Horse Council, 1700 K Street N.W.–Suite 300, Washington, D.C. 20006-3805; 202-296-4031. *Photographer's Market*, Writer's Digest Books, 1507 Dana Ave., Cincinnati, OH 45207.

RESEARCH SCIENTIST

Education: Ph.D. in animal science, equine nutrition, genetics, biochemistry, equine physiology, animal behavior, agricultural engineering, or related fields

Certification: None

Horse Experience: Not essential but helpful in understanding the needs of the industry and soliciting funds from horse organizations and businesses

Job Description: Research scientists search for answers to the horse industry's questions about optimum horse care, feeding, athletic stresses, feed production or processing, transportation methods, and many other topics where our knowledge is incomplete. They may work at an agricultural research facility located at one of the land-grant universities and be responsible for writing grant proposals to find funding for their projects, supervision of graduate students, and even teaching as well as performing their basic research. Other research scientists may be employees of a corporation responsible for carefully managing the company's research budget and disseminating information to other scientists, the company's sales staff, dealers, and the equine media. They work primarily indoors with little or no horse contact in their daily work. Hours are generally regular although some overtime without additional compensation is the norm for senior researchers. Corporate researchers generally earn more than university-level personnel.

Potential Earnings: Entry level—$25,000 to $40,000; after ten years—$50,000 to $75,000; top earnings—$80,000 to $100,000

Related Jobs: Equine nutritionist, university professor, extension horse agent

Making Contacts: Health and research organizations listed in *Horse Industry Directory*, American Horse Council, 1700 K Street N.W.—Suite 300, Washington, D.C. 20006-3805; 202-296-4031. Agricultural research facilities located at land-grant universities. Larger feed companies listed with the American Feed Industry Association, 1501 Wilson Blvd.—#1100, Arlington, VA 22209-2403; 703-524-0810. Professional organizations serving various scientific sub-groups.

RIDING INSTRUCTOR

Education: High school plus apprenticeship or other on-the-job training; trade school certificate, associate's or bachelor's degree in equine studies; or M.S. in equine studies, business, or education

Certification: American Riding Instructor Certification Program, P.O. Box 282, Alton Bay, NH 03810; 603-875-4000. Centered Riding® Inc., P.O. Box 2151, West Brattleboro, VT 05303; 802-254-2235. CHA, The Association For Horsemanship Safety, 5318 Old Bullard Road, Tyler, TX 75703; 800-399-0138. Horsemanship Safety Association, Drawer 30, Fentress, TX 78622; 800-798-8106. North American Riding for the Handicapped Association, P.O. Box 33150, Denver, CO 80233; 800-369-7433. United States Dressage Federation, P.O. Box 80668, Lincoln, NE 68501-0668; 402-434-8550.

Horse Experience: Competent riding and horse handling skills essential (the degree of riding excellence necessary increases as the level of riding competence taught advances); competitive experience highly desirable

Job Description: Riding instructors may teach rudimentary riding skills to beginners or coach Olympic riders on how to improve their already sophisticated skills. Most concentrate on one riding style or one sport in order to become as expert as possible in that area and create a marketing niche. Riding instruction involves not only solid riding skills but also excellent communication skills and an ability to organize progressive lesson programs that meet the needs of students. Riding instructors must know how to motivate and challenge people of all temperaments and levels of commitment. They enjoy daily horse contact, outdoor work, and a high degree of autonomy. Weekend work is constant. Some instructors work as employees and their duties may include stable management as well as instruction. They are generally paid a small salary plus a commission on the lessons they teach, and housing is sometimes provided. Other instructors are self-employed business people whose earnings depend on the number of lessons they give and the charge per lesson. Good marketing and business skills are as crucial to their success as solid writing and teaching ability. A survey by the American Riding Instructor's Certification Program found that, nationwide, their members were charging from $10 to $60 per hour for private lessons. Highly qualified instructors with a national reputation may charge up to $100 or more. Expenses for riding instructors can also be highly variable depending on whether they teach on student's horses, employer's horses, or their own string of school horses at their own or a rented facility. Most instructors cannot teach enough lessons to completely support themselves. They augment their income through clinics, coaching students at shows, farm sitting, farm management, training, judging, or other horse show assignments. Those earning a substantial portion of their income through clinics must be able to travel widely, have a clear and simple way of teaching fundamentals quickly, and be able to evaluate riders and horses quickly. The large number of part-time riding instructors tends to depress the income of anyone trying to teach full-time.

Potential Earnings: Highly variable: entry level—$0 to $5,000; after ten years—$12,000 to $20,000; top earnings—$25,000 to $60,000.

Related Jobs: Trainer, camp director, farm manager

Making Contacts: Directories listed by the certification programs listed above. Stables listed in local and regional horse directories. Classified ads in regional horse publications. Directories of national sport organizations listed in *Horse Industry Directory*, American Horse Council, 1700 K Street N.W.–Suite 300, Washington, D.C. 20006-3805; 202-296-4031. Equine employment agencies. Placement offices at schools with equine studies programs.

SADDLER, HARNESS MAKER

Education: High school plus apprenticeship or vocational school training

Certification: None

Horse Experience: Knowledge of riding or driving, competition rules, and horse anatomy very helpful in meeting customers' needs

Job Description: Saddlers and harness makers design, make, and repair horse tack. Some work as employees of large tack shops but most are self-employed business people working fairly regular hours with little direct contact with horses except for an occasional saddle fitting. Custom saddle and harness makers must have sharp marketing skills and know how to make the most efficient use of their working hours. That may mean hiring apprentices or assistants to help with certain aspects of the business that allow the craftsman to focus on what he does best. Independent personalities may find this hard. Some saddle and harness makers market only through word-of-mouth while others design long-term advertising strategies and take booths at major shows and trade fairs to keep their order books filled well into the future. A high commitment to quality and on-time delivery as well as an ability to design with flare without being outrageous are essential elements of success.

Potential Earnings: Entry level—$12,000 to $16,000; after ten years—$25,000 to $40,000; top earnings—$40,000 to $60,000; start-up costs for inventory, sewing machines, tools—$25,000 to $40,000

Related Jobs: Boot repair, tack shop sales, tack shop owner, manufacturer's sales representative

Making Contacts: *Tack 'N Togs Annual Buyers Guide*, P.O. Box 2400, 12400 Whitewater Drive–Suite 160, Minnetonka, MN 55343; 612-931-0211. W-E Source, 1226 W. Bayaud–Suite 300, Lakewood, CO 80228; 303-914-3000. *Harness Shop News*, Rte. 1 Box 212, Sylva, NC 28779.

TACK SHOP OWNER

Education: High school plus on-the-job experience or associate's or bachelor's degree in equine studies, animal science, economics, marketing, advertising, or business

Certification: None

Horse Experience: Solid horse experience essential to be able to stock correct inventory to meet customers' needs, answer

questions, and communicate well with people in the horse
industry

Job Description: Tack shop owners are the final link in the marketing chain from manufacturer to horse owner. Most shops
specialize in either English or Western lines and work diligently to stay abreast of trends in clothing, show tack, and other
products to keep inventory turning over. Tack shop owners
must become very knowledgeable about the equestrian specialties they supply in order to help customers make intelligent
buying decisions. They know satisfied customers will come
back. Bad advice will mean losing a customer. Tack shop owners must know how to buy and manage inventory, motivate
and supervise sales assistants, and market their store within the
region they serve. They work long, irregular hours including
many weekends. Their indoor jobs provide little direct contact
with horses. Fierce competition from large volume catalog dis-
counters able to buy at wholesale prices means tack shop
markups of 40 to 50 percent are far lower than those for other
types of retail stores. That means it takes longer to recoup
start-up costs for new businesses.

Potential Earnings: Entry level—$0 to $20,000; after ten years—
$35,000 to $50,000; top earnings—$45,000 to $100,000;
start-up costs for inventory, store fixtures, etc.—$50,000 to
$75,000

Related Jobs: Manufacturer's sales representative, wholesale distributor, saddle and/or harness maker

Making Contacts: *International Saddlery and Apparel Journal*, 1130
Guynn, Paint Lick, KY 40461; 603-437-3400. *Tack 'N Togs
Annual Buyers Guide*, P.O. Box 2400, 12400 Whitewater
Drive–Suite 160, Minnetonka, MN 55343; 612-931-0211.

TRAILER SALES AGENT

Education: High school plus sales experience; associate's or bachelor's degree in animal science, equine studies, marketing, or
business

Certification: None

Horse Experience: Familiarity with horses, the stresses of traveling with horses, and the horse show scene fosters empathy
with customer's needs; familiarity with a particular breed or
sport discipline helps when marketing trailers to horsemen in
those breeds or disciplines

Job Description: Trailer sales personnel help horsemen making buying decisions about transportation for their horses. Using a line of credit from a bank or other lender, they purchase trailers for resale, display them on a lot, and advertise for customers. Only a few dealers make a full-time living from trailer sales; most sell only one or two trailers monthly as a sideline to other business endeavors. They typically realize 15 percent of the trailer's sale price as gross profits. Then they must deduct expenses. Expenses are high in this business because the dealer must buy or rent a lot to display the trailers, spend a great deal of time with potential buyers educating them about the good and bad points of various kinds of trailer design and construction, and advertise heavily to bring customers to the lot. Trailer sales personnel work both indoors and outdoors and seldom have daily contact with horses. Hours can be irregular and weekend hours are a necessity.

Potential Earnings: Entry level—$0 to $20,000; after ten years—$20,000 to $40,000; top earnings—$60,000 to $100,000 (for high volume, full-time trailer sales; much less for all others)

Related Jobs: Truck sales, body shop owner, welding shop operator

Making Contacts: National Association of Trailer Manufacturers, La Costs Green Office Bldg., 1033 La Pasad Dr.–Suite 200, Austin, TX 78752; 512-454-8626. Local and regional horse directories and publications.

TRAINER

Education: High school plus on-the-job training; vocational school, associate's degree, or bachelor's degree in equine science with emphasis on training techniques; business courses helpful

Certification: State licensing exams for Thoroughbred racehorse trainers; none for others

Horse Experience: Extensive knowledge of horse behavior, training methods, conditioning

Job Description: Trainers prepare horses to be useful companions and compete in athletic endeavors. Some part-time riding horse trainers may go to clients' barns to work with horses but most trainers work out of a base facility and clients bring their horses there. "Training board" is higher than regular board, reflecting the cost of the trainer's services. Like riding instructors, trainers may augment their income through clinics and also earn fees coaching clients at competitions. Trainers work

long hours, and during competition seasons they work seven days a week training at home and attending shows on weekends. As self-employed business owners, their income depends on the number of horses in their care and their ability to control expenses. Thoroughbred racehorse trainers must know how to properly condition a racing athlete and evaluate its ability so that it is entered in the proper races. They receive a portion of any purses their charges win on top of the training board they charge owners.

Potential Earnings: Entry level—$8,000 to $12,000; after ten years—$25,000 to $40,000; top earnings—$60,000 to $75,000

Related Jobs: Riding instructor, farm manager, professional rider

Making Contacts: Local and regional horse directories and horse publications. United Thoroughbred Trainers of America, 19800 W. Nine Mile Rd., Southfield, MI 48075-3960; 810-354-3232.

TRANSPORTATION DRIVER

Education: High school plus on-the-job experience

Certification: Class A or B commercial driver's license

Horse Experience: Understanding of horse behavior and safety procedures, solid general horse knowledge highly desirable

Job Description: Horse van and truck drivers carry horses from their home base to competitions all over the country. Some even fly as attendants with horses traveling overseas. They must not only know how to drive in a manner that provides the greatest margin of comfort and safety for the horse; they must also know how to minimize stress during loading and unloading and be ready to handle travel emergencies. Most are salaried employees whose work hours can be very irregular. Commercial drivers seeking jobs may be subject to drug and alcohol testing and must have a clean driving record.

Potential Earnings: Entry level—$18,000 to $22,000; after ten years—$30,000 to $40,000; top earnings—$50,000

Related Jobs: Farm manager, assistant trainer, groom

Making Contacts: Local and regional directories. Animal Transportation Association, P.O. Box 3565, North Potomac, MD 20885-3565; 301-998-6343. *Who's Who in Live Animal Trade and Transport*, P.O. Box 441110, Ft. Washington, MD 20749; 301-292-1970.

UNIVERSITY PROFESSOR

Education: Ph.D. in animal science, equine nutrition, genetics, biochemistry, equine physiology, animal behavior, agricultural engineering, or related fields

Certification: None

Horse Experience: Not essential but helpful when applying academic knowledge to real management situations

Job Description: University professors and other college-level instructors educate successive generations of horsemen and other workers in the animal industry. They must organize lesson plans, give lectures, and provide hands-on practical labs to give their students depth of knowledge. Through testing and grading they offer feedback to students. Many professors also supervise student activities such as horse clubs, intercollegiate rodeo or horse show training, and livestock judging. Professors are also expected to do a certain amount of writing and publishing in academic journals. Depending on their academic specialty, they may have little or no direct contact with horses or they may work with horses daily. Their hours are very irregular, often including evenings and weekends, but university personnel report a high level of satisfaction from professional recognition and the stimulation of constant contact with young people and fresh ideas.

Potential Earnings: Entry level $20,000 to 40,000; after ten years—$40,000 to $60,000; top earnings—$60,000 to $80,000

Related Jobs: Extension agent, research scientist

Making Contacts: *Horse Industry Directory*, American Horse Council, 1700 K Street N.W.–Suite 300, Washington, D.C. 20006-3805; 202-296-4031. Land-grant universities.

VETERINARIAN - FEDERAL OR STATE

Education: D.V.M. (four years of pre-veterinary studies plus four years of veterinary school)

Certification: State veterinary board exam, civil service exam

Horse Experience: Solid general knowledge of horse management and behavior highly desirable

Job Description: Government veterinarians enforce animal protection laws, work to prevent and control the spread of contagious diseases among animals or from animals to humans, and design research projects on animal diseases. They form the front line in preventing foreign diseases from gaining a foothold on United States shores. A large number of veterinarians work to keep our human food supply chain untainted. They work in the U.S. Department of Agriculture, the Food and Drug Administration, the U.S. Public Health Service, and the U.S. Army. Government veterinarians are salaried employees whose work is almost always performed indoors. Most have little or no direct contact with horses. Those in administrative positions need personnel management skills as well as excellent communications skills.

Potential Earnings: Entry level—$35,000 to $40,000; after ten years—$50,000 to $60,000; top earnings—$70,000 to $100,000

Related Jobs: Research veterinarian, industrial veterinarian, private practice veterinarian, university professor, researcher

Making Contacts: American Veterinary Medical Association, 1931 Meacham Rd.–#100, Schaumburg, IL 60173-4360; 708-925-8070. American Association of Equine Practitioners, 4075 Ironworks Pike, Lexington, KY 40511-8434; 606-233-0147. U.S. Department of Agriculture, Animal and Plant Health Inspection Service, Hyattsville, MD 20782. Food and Drug Administration, Center for Veterinary Medicine, Rockville, MD 20857.

VETERINARIAN - CORPORATE

Education: D.V.M. (four years of pre-veterinary studies plus four years of veterinary school); often additional study in equine nutrition, physiology, toxicology, or other specialties

Certification: State veterinary board exams; board specialty exams

Horse Experience: Highly desirable in order to understand the potential application of products in the equestrian marketplace

Job Description: Corporate veterinarians work for large pharmaceutical and feed companies, helping to develop and test new products for the equine industry. They also become involved with educating a company's sales force about such products as pharmaceuticals or feed supplements to indirectly disseminate that knowledge to horsemen. Veterinarians employed by racetracks or by a single large farm fall into the category of corporate veterinarians because they are salaried and work fairly regular hours compared to their counterparts in private practice. Corporate veterinarians are seldom hired right out of school. Usually they are veterinarians with many years of experience in private practice who have made a career change.

Potential Earnings: Entry level—$60,000 to $65,000; after ten years—$80,000 to $100,000; top earnings—$100,000

Related Jobs: Research veterinarian, government veterinarian, private practice veterinarian, university professor, researcher, equine nutritionist

Making Contacts: American Veterinary Medical Association, 1931 Meacham Rd.–#100, Schaumburg, IL 60173-4360; 708-925-8070. American Association of Equine Practitioners, 4075 Ironworks Pike, Lexington, KY 40511-8434; 606-233-0147.

VETERINARIAN - PRIVATE PRACTICE

Education: D.V.M. (four years of pre-veterinary studies plus four years of veterinary school)

Certification: State veterinary board examination

Horse Experience: Solid horse handling skills and a good understanding of horse behavior

Job Description: Veterinarians in private practice provide medical attention to horses within their geographic area over a long day that can begin early in the morning and run until early evening. Weekend work is the norm. Their days are filled with examinations, inoculations, radiographs, evaluations, surgeries, and sometimes small triumphs when their patients improve against the odds. Veterinarians must not only have excellent diagnostic skills and be current about the latest treatment; they must also have good communication skills to help owners understand their horse's medical problem and their role in administering medications or other continuing treatment. Graduate veterinarians usually work as employees (or associates) with an established private practice for several years to gain experience. Then they may be asked to join the practice as a partner. As partners, the veterinarians are all small business operators who must carefully watch expenses including the mortgage on their clinic, insurance, office personnel, medical inventory, trucks, and more.

Potential Earnings: Entry level—$20,000 to $30,000; after ten years—$50,000 to $60,000; top earnings—$80,000 to $100,000

Related Jobs: Research veterinarian, government veterinarian, corporate veterinarian, veterinary technician

Making Contacts: American Veterinary Medical Association, 1931 Meacham Rd.–#100, Schaumburg, IL 60173-4360; 708-

925-8070. American Association of Equine Practitioners, 4075
Ironworks Pike, Lexington, KY 40511-8434;
606-233-0147.

VETERINARY TECHNICIAN

Education: Associate's or bachelor's degree in veterinary technology or related field

Certification: Certification or licensing required in about two thirds of the states

Horse Experience: Good general knowledge of horses essential whether working for a private practice vet or in other capacities where equine knowledge will be helpful in communicating with customers

Job Description: Veterinary technicians perform a broad range of functions throughout the horse industry. Their most obvious role is as a professional assistant to a veterinarian on his rounds and with office paperwork. Vet techs help set up radiology equipment, hold horses during procedures, act as surgical nurses, and help care for hospitalized animals. They enjoy daily contact with horses, and their hours tend to be long but fairly predictable. Veterinary technicians also work in the corporate world as sales representatives, educators, diagnostic technicians, and research assistants. Corporate vet techs enjoy regular working hours and good job benefits but seldom come in direct contact with horses.

Potential Earnings: Entry level—$15,000 to $17,000; after ten years—$18,000 to $20,000; top earnings—$20,000 to $24,000

Related Jobs: Manufacturer's sales representative, humane investigator, lab technician

Making Contacts: North American Veterinary Technician Association, P.O. Box 224, Battle Ground, IN 47920; 217-351-2418.

VIDEOGRAPHER

Education: Bachelor's degree in fine arts or a field related to your video specialty such as equine studies or animal science, with additional courses in marketing and business

Certification: None

Horse Experience: Not essential but an understanding of how horses behave and move

Job Description: Videographers work at two levels in the horse industry. Some attend horse shows to record horse performances for owners to review. They also go to farms to produce sales videos used to market horses. A good videographer must know how to frame and follow action smoothly and move seamlessly from scene to scene. Other videographers produce educational films for mass distribution. These need careful scripting, sometimes require working with a professional writer, and are often given musical accompaniments. Dozens of videocassettes will be edited into a single thirty-minute or 60-minute production; then hundreds of copies must be made and marketed. The videographer may be paid a flat fee for producing the tape or may produce and market tapes himself as a small business person. Either way, a videographer must wield a sharp pencil to keep expenses at a minimum and bring profits to the bottom line. Established videographers say newcomers should have a savings cushion two to three times the amount they need to live on and be prepared for several very lean years until they develop a reputation and a client base. Most videographers do not make their living exclusively by shooting horses but also by shooting weddings or other events or by creating and mass marketing videos in other fields.

Potential Earnings: Entry level—$0 to $10,000; after ten years—$18,000 to $25,000; top earnings—$40,000 to $60,000; start-up costs—$15,000 for cameras, lenses, editing equipment, copying equipment, etc. for a show/farm photographer to $100,000 or more for video producer doing mass marketing

Related Jobs: Photographer

Making Contacts: *Horse Industry Directory*, American Horse Council, 1700 K Street N.W.–Suite 300, Washington, D.C. 20006-3805; 202-296-4031. Local and regional horse publications and directories. Lists of shows and show managers from sport organizations.

WHOLESALE DISTRIBUTOR

Education: Four-year degree in marketing, business, or a field—such as equine studies, animal science or agriculture—relating to the products you plan to sell

Certification: None

Horse Experience: Solid knowledge of the horse industry and its needs important to success in stocking and moving inventory

Job Description: Wholesale distributors are part of the marketing pipeline carrying goods from manufacturers to retail buyers. Within a defined region or territory, distributors represent product lines from several national companies which may or may not give them exclusive rights to represent the company in that territory. Distributors buy goods in very large quantities at the manufacturer's lowest price. They then resell the products to retail outlets or sometimes directly to retail buyers with the difference between their buying price and selling price determining company profits and earnings. Wholesalers must have good business skills to manage inventory, market to buyers, and supervise personnel. Their businesses keep them primarily indoors with little direct horse contact.

Potential Earnings: Entry level—$0 to $30,000; after ten years—$40,000 to $80,000; top earnings—$80,000 to $120,000

Related Jobs: Manufacturer's sales representative, retail tack shop owner, catalog seller

Making Contacts: *International Saddlery and Apparel Journal*, 1130 Guynn, Paint Lick, KY 40461; 606-986-3044. *Tack 'N Togs Annual Buyers Guide*, P.O. Box 2400, 12400 Whitewater Drive–Suite 160, Minnetonka, MN 55343; 612-931-0211. W-E Source, 1226 W. Bayaud, Suite 300, Lakewood, CO 80228; 303-914-3000.

WRANGLER

Education: High school, trade school

Certification: In western states, packers and guides may need permits for pack trips on federally owned lands

Horse Experience: Excellent knowledge of horse care and horse behavior essential to keep animals sound, ensure proper tack fit, and handle back country emergencies when a veterinarian is not available

Job Description: Some wranglers work for packers and guides providing back country experiences for riders of all ages and walks of life. Their work tends to be seasonal, taking families, fishermen, nature lovers, and horsemen into mountainous back country for camping trips during the summer months or hunting parties in the fall. They must be alert, able to think on their feet in adverse situations, and be able to work well with all types of people since their clients change weekly. Other wranglers work at dude ranches caring for the strings of horses ridden by guests and leading daily or overnight rides. Wranglers work very hard during the short season when their ser-

vices are in demand. The work involves hours in the saddle and is almost entirely outdoors, whatever the weather. More and more, wranglers must also be environmentally aware, seeking ways to minimize the impact of horses and campers on back country campsites to preserve the wilderness for future generations of riders and prevent pressures from groups seeking to limit or abolish horse travel in wilderness and other back country areas.

Potential Earnings: Entry level—$500 to $800 per month during the season plus tips; after ten years—$1,000 to $1,500 monthly; top earnings—$1,500 monthly

Related Jobs: Packer, guide, dude ranch operator

Making Contacts: Dude Ranchers Association, P.O. Box 471, LaPorte, CO 80535; 303-493-7623. Colorado Dude and Guest Ranch Association, P.O. Box 300, Tabernash, CO 80478; 303-887-3128. America Outdoors, P.O. Box 1348, Knoxville, TN 37901; 615-524-4814. Equine employment agencies.

WRITER

Education: Four-year degree in English, journalism, agricultural journalism, or related fields

Certification: None

Horse Experience: Intimate knowledge of horses and the horse industry is something you must have or know how to thoroughly research to appeal to a very knowledgeable and generally well-read audience

Job Description: Equine writers cover horse events, interview experts, and ferret out the newest information from companies, equine professionals, researchers, and others to educate and entertain the readers of horse publications. Except for magazine staff writers, equine writers are self-employed business people who are paid by the article. Payments may range from nothing but a by-line to $400 or occasionally more. Writers must constantly work to develop contacts for stories and market ideas to editors in hopes of landing assignments. Today's publishing world demands that writers be computer-literate and able to communicate with publications by disk, fax, and modem. The large number of part-time writers and horse professionals offering free editorial copy to horse publications in exchange for the free publicity they receive makes it difficult to work full-time as an equine writer without supplementing your income from other writing sources.

Potential Earnings: Entry level—$0 to $5,000; after ten years—$10,000 to $18,000; top earnings $30,000 to $40,000 (equine writing alone); start-up costs for computer, fax, modem, phone lines, copying machine, business stationary, etc.—$2,000 to $5,000

Related Jobs: Editor, publisher, marketing or public relations professional

Making Contacts: Horse publications listed in *Horse Industry Directory*, American Horse Council, 1700 K Street N.W.—Suite 300, Washington, D.C. 20006-3805; 202-296-4031. American Horse Publications, 2946 Carriage Dr., South Daytona, FL 32119; 904-760-7743. National Turf Writers Association, 1314 Bentwood Way, Louisville, KY 40223; 502-245- 3809. United States Harness Writers Association, P.O. Box 10, Batavia, NY 14021-0010. *Writer's Market*, Writer's Digest Books, 1507 Dana Ave., Cincinnati, OH 45207.

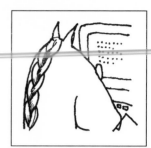

HUNTSMAN

Like huntsmen for generations before her, Rhoda Hopkins learned her craft through apprenticeship. For 20 years, Rhoda and her late husband rode with the Golden's Bridge hounds in North Salem, New York. After her husband's death, she served as a whipper-in to huntsman Donald Philtower. She credits him for teaching her the finer points of working with hounds.

Huntsmen must not only know horses and hounds, they must be a jack-of-all-trades around the kennel and good at public relations. One of their most important jobs is to maintain cordial relations with landowners whose properties are open to the hunt. The huntsman also builds and repairs jumps throughout the hunt's territory. Good hounds are the soul of the hunt, and a huntsman must study bloodlines, recommend breedings, and keep alert to the possibilities of bringing new genetic material into the pack from other kennels. It is the huntsman who trains the young whelps, instilling discipline without crushing initiative. The huntsman and his or her staff also care for their own and any other mounts maintained by the hunt for guests.

Rhoda hunted a pack of Penn-Marydel hounds for the Fairfield County Hounds in Bridgewater, Connecticut, for over fifteen years and now hunts both crossbred hounds and beagles as huntsman for the Old Chatham Hunt in Malden Bridge, New York. There are some people who have a knack for working with hounds, she says, and others who can work with them for years and never develop a real rapport. Rhoda believes a huntsman must have the ability to listen and observe so that he or she begins to think and feel like a hound. "I don't think anyone could step into a huntsman's job having just read a book about foxhunting," she says.

Rhoda's day begins a 4:30 a.m. when she gets up to do paperwork, tidy the house provided as part of her compensation from the hunt, feed the horses, and collect eggs from her chickens. By 6 a.m. she is in the kennels to feed the hounds, and kennel cleaning occupies her time until about 8 a.m. The

rest of the day might be spent on a tractor mowing swaths at the edges of fields, bumping across country in her truck (also provided as part of her compensation package) to repair panels and coops, or roading hounds to condition them for the hunt season. During hunting season, she hunts the hounds twice a week, and in spring there are hound shows to prepare for. Rhoda also gets medical benefits and a pension plan through the Masters of Foxhounds Association. Despite her long hours and hard work, Rhoda cannot imagine any other lifestyle. "You're talking to a happy huntsman who's very enthusiastic about every aspect of the job." ■

Appendix

SCHOOL ADDRESSES

Alabama A&M University
Normal, AL 35762

Alcorn State University
Lorman, MS 39096

Alfred University
Equine Studies RD 1
P.O. Box 265
Angelica, NY 14709

Allen County Community College
Equine Studies
1801 North Cottonwood
Iola, KS 66749

Auburn University
Animal Science Building—Room 212
Auburn, AL 36849-5528

Averett College
Equestrian Studies Coordinator
Danville, VA 24541

Becker College—Leicester Campus
Animal Care Studies
3 Paxton St.
Leicester, MA 01524

Berry College
Animal Science Department
P.O. Box 357
Mount Berry, GA 30149-0326

Black Forest Hall
Equestrian Studies
Quick and Hoyt Roads
P.O. Box 140
Harbor Springs, MI 49740

Black Hawk College
East Campus Horse Science—#264
1501 Illinois Highway 78
Kewanee, IL 61443

Blue Ridge Community College
Animal Science Studies
P.O. Box 80
Weyers Cave, VA 24486

Brigham Young University
Equine Studies
101 EMLC
Provo, UT 84602

Brookdale Community College
Equine Studies
Newman Springs Rd.
Lincroft, NJ 07738

C.S. Mott Community College
711 North Saginaw Street
Flint, MI 48503

California Polytechnic State University
Animal Science Department
3801 W. Temple Ave.
Pomona, CA 91768

California State University - Fresno
Animal Science Department
Fresno, CA 93740-0075

Camden County College
Animal Science Technology Program
P.O. Box 200
Blackwood, NJ 08012

Canadian School of Horseshoeing
RR 2
Guelph, Ontario N1H 6H8
Canada

Casey and Son Horseshoeing School
14013 East Hwy 136
Lafayette, GA 30728

Cazenovia College
Director - Equine Studies Program
Cazenovia, NY 13035

Cecil Community College
Equine Studies
1000 North East Rd.
North East, MD 21901

Cedar Valley College
Veterinary Technology Program
3030 N. Dallas Avenue
Lancaster, TX 75134

Centenary College
Equine Studies Division
400 Jefferson St.
Hackettstown, NJ 07840

Central Carolina Community College
1105 Kelly Drive
Sanford, NC 27330

Central Florida Community College
Equine Studies
400 Jefferson St.
Hackettstown, NJ 07840

Central Texas College
Equine Studies
P.O. Box 1800
Killeen, TX 76540

Central Wyoming College
Equine Studies
Riverton, WY 82501

Cheff Center for the Handicapped
8450 N. 43rd Street
P.O. Box 368
August, MI 49012

Clemson University
Animal Science Department
Clemson, SC 29634

Colby Community College
Equine Studies
1255 South Range
Colby, KS 67701

Colby-Sawyer College
Equine Studies
New London, NH 03257

College of Southern Idaho
Coordinator of Equine Studies
Box 744
Twin Falls, ID 83301

College of the Redwoods
Equine Studies
7351 Tompkins Hill Rd.
Eureka, CA 95501

Colorado Mountain College
Veterinary Technology Program
Coordinator of Veterinary Studies
3000 County Road 114
Glenwood Springs, CO 81601

Colorado School of Trades
1575 Hoyt Street
Lakewood, CO 80215

Colorado State University
Equine Sciences Program
Fort Collins, CO 80523

Columbia State Community College
Veterinary Technology Program
Columbia, TN 38401

Columbus State Community College
550 E. Spring Street
Columbus, OH 43216

Connors State College
Equine Studies Box 706
Warner, OK 74469

Consumnes River College
Animal Health Technology Program
8401 Center Parkway
Sacramento, CA 95823

Cornell University
Animal Science Department
346 Morrison
Ithaca, NY 14853

Dawson Community College
Equine Studies
P.O. Box 421
Glendive, MT 59330

Del-Rea Institute of Animal Technology
1681 S. Dayton St.
Denver, CO 80231

Delaware State College
Dover, DE 19901

Delaware Valley College of Science and Agriculture
Equine Studies
700 East Butler Ave.
Doylestown, PA 18901

Dodge City Community College
Equine Studies
2501 N. 14th Ave.
Dodge City, KS 67801

Eastern School of Farriery
P.O. Box 1368
Martinsville, VA 24114

Eastern Wyoming College
Veterinary Technology Program
3200 West C. St.
Torrington, WY 82240

Elms College
Equine Studies
291 Springfield St.
Chicopee, MA 01013

Equine Sports Massage Program
14735 SW 71 Ave. Rd.
Ocala, FL 34473

Equissage
P.O. Box 2167
Southern Pines, NC 28388

EquiTouch Systems
8109 Watt Ave. #172
Antelope, CA 95843

Essex Community College
Veterinary Technology Program
7201 Rossville Blvd.
Baltimore, MD 21237

Fairmont State College
Veterinary Technology Program
Fairmont, WV 26554

Far Hills Forge
Master Farrier
P.O. Box 703
Far Hills, NJ 07931

Feather River College
Equine Studies
P.O. Box 11110
Quincy, CA 95971

Ferrum College
Equine Center Equine Studies
Ferrum, VA 24088

Florida A&M University
Tallahassee, FL 32307

Florida School of Horseshoeing
P.O. Box 423
Belleville, MI 48111

Foothill College Animal Health Technology Program
12345 El Monte Rd.
Los Altos Hills, CA 94022

Fort Valley State College
Veterinary Technology Program
Fort Valley, GA 31030

Green River Community College
Equine Studies
12401 S.E. 320th St.
Auburn, WA 98002

Gulf Coast Farriers School
2701 Mustang Rd.
Alvin, TX 77511

Harcum Junior College
Equine Studies
Bryn Mawr, PA 19010

Hartnell College
Animal Health Technology Program
156 Homestead Ave.
Salina, CA 939001

Hawkeye Hill Racing School
RR #1 Box 382
Commiskey, IN 47227

Hinds Community College
Veterinary Technology Program
P.O. Box 10461
Raymond, MS 39154

Hiwassee College
Equine Studies
P.O. Box 623
Madisonville, TN 37354

Holyoke Community College
Veterinary & Animal Science Career Program
303 Homestead Ave.
Holyoke, MA 01040-1099

Illinois Valley Community College
Equine Studies
2578 E. 350th Road
Oglesby, IL 61348-1099

Iowa State University
Animal Science Department
119 Kildee
Ames, IA 50011

Iowa State University
College of Veterinary Medicine
Ames, IA 50011

Jefferson College
1000 Viking Drive
Hillsboro, MO 63050

Johnson County Community College
Equine Studies
12345 College Blvd. at Quivira
Overland Park, KS 66210

Johnson & Wales University
Department of Equine Studies
8 Abbott Park Place
Providence, RI 02903

Judson College
Equine Science Studies
Marion, AL 36756

Kansas State University
College of Veterinary Medicine
Associate Dean's Office
Manhattan, KS 66506

Kansas State University
Manhattan, KS 66506

Kemptville College of Agricultural Technology
Equine Studies
P.O. Box 2003 Prescott Street
Kemptville, Ontario KOG1JO
Canada

Kentucky Horse Park Education Dept.
4089 Iron Works Pike
Lexington, KY 40511

Kentucky Horseshoeing School
P.O. Box 120
Hwy 53
Mount Eden, KY 40046

Kentucky State University
Frankfort, KY 40601

King's River Community College
Equine Studies
995 N. Reed
Reedley, CA 93654

Kirkwood Community College
Veterinary Technology Program
6301 Kirkwood Blvd. S.W.
Cedar Rapids, IA 52406

Kwantlen College
Langley Campus
P.O. Box 9030
Surrey, British Columbia V3T 5H8
Canada

La Guardia Community College
The City University of New York
31-10 Thomson Avenue
Long Island City, NY 11101

Lake Erie College
Equine Studies Department
391 W. Washington St.
LEC Box 345
Painesville, OH 44077

Lakeshore Technical College
Equine Studies
1290 North Avenue
Cleveland, WI 53015

Lamar Community College
Equine Studies
2401 South Main St.
Lamar, CO 81052

Langston University
Langston, OK 73050

Laramie County Community College
1400 East College Drive
Cheyenne, WY 82007

Lassen College
Equine Studies
714-825 Sagebrush Blvd.
Susanville, CA 96130

Lincoln Memorial University
Veterinary Technology Program
Harrogate, TN 37752

Lincoln University
Jefferson City, MO 65101

Linn-Benton Community College
6500 SW Pacific Blvd.
Albany, OR 97321

Lookout Mountain School of Horseshoeing
Rt. 8, Box 277
400 Lewis Rd.
Gadsden, AL 35901

Lord Fairfax Community College
Equine Studies
P.O. Box 47
Middletown, VA 22645

Los Angeles Pierce College
Animal Health Technology Program
6201 Winnetka Ave.
Woodland Hills, CA 91371

Louisiana State University
Animal Science Department
105 J.B. Francioni Building
Baton Rouge, LA 70803

Louisiana Tech University
Animal Science Department
P.O. Box 10198
Ruston, LA 71272

Macomb Community College
Veterinary Technician Program
44575 Garfield Rd.
Mt. Clemens, MI 48044

Madison Area Technical College
Veterinary Technology Program
3550 Anderson
Madison, WI 53704

Manor Junior College
Veterinary Technology Program
Fox Chase Road & Forest Avenue
Jenkintown, PA 19046

Maple Woods Community College
2601 N.E. Barry Road
Kansas City, MO 64156

Martin Community College
Equine Technologies Department
1161 Kehukee Park Rd.
Williamston, NC 27892

Medical Institute of Minnesota
Veterinary Technician Program
5503 Green Valley Drive
Bloomington, MN 55437

Merced College
3600 M St.
Merced, CA 95340

Mercy College
555 Broadway
Dobbs Ferry, NY 10522

Meredith Manor International Equestrian Centre
Route 1 Box 66FJ
Waverly, WV 26184

Mesa Technical College
Box 1143
Tucumcari, NM 88401

Michigan School of Horseshoeing
P.O. Box 423
Belleville, MI 48111

Michigan State University
Department of Animal Science
124 Anthony Hall
East Lansing, MI 48824-1225

Middle Tennessee State University
Animal Science Department
Murfreesboro, TN 37132

Midland College
Veterinary Technology Program
3000 N. Garland
Midland, TX 79705

Midway College
Chairman of Equine Studies
512 East Stephens St.
Midway, KY 40347-1120

Midwest Horseshoeing School
2312 South Maple Ave.
Macomb, IL 61455

Minnesota School of Horseshoeing
6250 Riverdale Drive NW
Ramsey, MN 55303

Mississippi State University
Animal & Dairy Science
Box 9815
Mississippi State, MS 39762

Montana State University
Animal Science Department
119 Linfield Hall
Bozeman, MT 406-994-2648

Morehead State University
Animal Science Department
P.O. Box 702 25
MSU Farm Drive
Morehead, KY 40351

Mount Ida College
Equine Studies
777 Dedham St.
Newton Center, MA 02159

Mount Senario College
Equine Studies
1500 College Ave. West
Ladysmith, WI 54848

Mt. San Antonio College
Animal Health Technology Program
1100 N. Grand Ave.
Walnut, CA 91789

Murray State University
Animal Science Department
Murray, KY 42071

National College
Allied Health Division
321 Kansas City Street
Rapid City, SD 57709

Nebraska College of Technical Agriculture
Curtis, NE 69025

New Mexico State University
Animal Science Department
Box 3-1
Las Cruces, NM 30003

North Carolina A&T State University
Greensboro, NC 27420

North Carolina State University
Department of Animal Science
Box 7621
Raleigh, NC 27695-7621

North Central Texas College
Equine Studies
1525 West California
Gainesville, TX 76240

North Dakota State University
Department of Veterinary Science
Fargo, ND 58105

North Texas Farrier's School
P.O. Box 666
Mineral Wells, TX 76068

Northeast Louisiana University
Animal Science Department
Monroe, LA 71209-0510

Northeast Missouri State University
Horse Program Leader
158 Barnett Hall
Kirksville, MO 63501

Northeastern Junior College
Equine Studies
100 College Drive
Sterling, CO 80751-2399

Northern Virginia Community College
Veterinary Technology Program
Loudoun Campus
1000 Harry Flood Byrd Highway
Sterling, VA 22170

Northwest College
Equine Studies
231 West 6th St.
Powell, WY 82435-1898

Northwest Missouri State University
Animal Science Department
Maryville, MO 64468

Northwestern State Univeristy of Louisiana
Department of Cooperative Programs & Agriculture
Williamson Hall—Room 218
Natchitoches, LA 71497

Ogonz Equestrian Center
R.D. #1
Lisbon, NH 03585

Ohio State University
Department of Animal Science
1800 Cannon Drive
Columbus, OH 43210

Ohio State University
Agricultural & Technical Institute
Equine Studies
1328 Dover Rd.
Wooster, OH 44691

Oklahoma Farrier's College, Inc.
Route 2—Box 88
Sperry, OK 74073

Oklahoma Horseshoeing School
3000 North Interstate 35
Oklahoma City, OK 73111

Oklahoma State Horseshoeing School
Route 1—Box 28-B
Ardmore, OK 73401

Oklahoma State University
Department of Animal Science
Stillwater, OK 74078-0102

Oklahoma State University-Technical Branch
Shoe-Boot-Saddle Department
Okmulgee, OK 74447

Olds College
Olds, Alberta T0M 1P0
Canada

Omaha College of Health Careers
10845 Harney
Omaha, NE 68154

Oregon State University
OSU Horse Center
Corvallis, OR 97331-6702

Otterbein College
Department of Equine Science
Westerville, OH 43081

Pace University
Director of Equine Studies
Box 3-1
Pleasantville, NY 10570-2799

Pacific Coast Horseshoeing School
9625 Florin Rd.
Sacramento, CA 95829

Parkland College
Veterinary Technology Program
2400 W. Bradley Ave.
Champaign IL 61821

Pennsylvania State University
Animal Science Department
324 Hemming Building
University Park, PA 16802

Pierce College at Fort Steilacoom
Veterinary Technology Program
9401 Farwest Dr. SW
Tacoma, WA 98498

Pike's Peak Community College
Farrier Program
1528 Turner Road
Colorado Springs, CO 80920

Portland Community College
Veterinary Technology Program
P.O. Box 19000
Portland, OR 97219

Prairie View A&M University
Prairie View, TX 77446-2867

Purdue University
Department of Animal Sciences
1026 Poultry Bldg.
West Lafayette, IN 47907-7677

Quinnipiac College
Veterinary Technology Program
Mt. Carmel Ave. P.O. Box 125
Hamden, CT 06518

Rancho Del Castillo
3708 Crystal Beach Rd.
Winter Haven, FL 33880

Rawhide Vocational College
Equine Studies
Lilac Rd.
Bonsall, CA 92003

Raymond Walters College
Animal Health Technology Program
University of Cincinnati
Cincinnati, OH 45221

Redlands Community College
Equine Studies
2501 N. 14th Ave.
El Reno, OK 73036

Rocky Mountain College
Equine Studies
1511 Poly Drive
Billings, MT 59102

Rogers State College
Director of Horse & Ranch Management
Claremore, OK 74017

Rush's Lakeview Outfitter and Guide School
Monida Star Route
Lima, MT 59739

Rutgers University
Cook College
P.O. Box 231
New Brunswick, NJ 08903-0231

Saint Mary-of-the-Woods College
Equine Studies
Saint Mary-of-the-Woods, IN 47846-1099

Salem-Teikyo University
Equine Careers and Industry Mgmnt. Dept.
P.O. Box 500
Salem, WV 26426

San Diego Mesa College
Animal Health Technology Program
7520 Mesa College Dr.
San Diego, CA 92111

Scottsdale Community College
Equine Studies Program
9000 East Chaparral Road
Scottsdale, AZ 85250

Seneca College of Applied Arts & Technology
Farrier Program
13390 Dufferin St. N
King City, Ontario L0G 1K0
Canada

Shasta College
Equine Studies
1065 N. Old Oregon Trail
P.O. Box 496006
Redding, CA 96049

Sheridan College
Animal Science Department
Box 5100
Sheridan, WY 82801

Shur Shod Shoeing School
Box 119
Cimarron, KS 67835

Sierra College
Equine Studies
5000 Rocklin Road
Rocklin, CA 95677-3397

Sierra Equestrian
Route 1
Rocking K
Bishop, CA 93514

Snead State Community College
Veterinary Technology Program
Boaz, AL 35957

South Carolina State College
Orangeburg, SC 29117

South Dakota State University
Animal Science Department
Box 2170
Brookings, SD 57007

South Puget Sound Community College
Farrier Program
2011 Mottman Road SW
Olympia, WA 98502

Southern Illinois University–Carbondale
Animal Science Department
Carbondale, IL 62901

Southern University and A&M College
Baton Rouge, LA 70813

Southern Virgnia College for Women
Equine Studies
One College Hill Dr.
Buena Vista, VA 24416

Southwest Missouri State University
Animal Science Department
901 S. National Ave.
Springfield, MO 65802

St. Andrews Presbyterian College
Equine Studies Department
8088 Mcleod Rd.
Laurinburg, NC 28352

St. Petersburg Junior College
Veterinary Technology Program
Box 13489
St. Petersburg, FL 33733

State University of New York–Canton
Canton, NY 13617

State University of New York–Cobleskill
Animal Science Department
Cobleskil,l NY 12043

State University of New York–Delhi
Department of Equine Science
Delhi, NY 13753

State University of New York–Morrisville
Animal Husbandry Department
Marshall Hall
Morrisville, NY 13408

State University of New York–Farmingdale
Farmingdale, NY 11735

Stephens College
Equestrian Studies
Box 2071
Columbia, MO 65215

Sul Ross State University
Range Animal Science Program
Box C-110
Alpine, TX 79832

Tarlton State University
Stephensville, TX 76402

Teikyo Post University
Director of Equine Programs
800 Country Club Rd.
P.O. Box 2540
Waterbury, CT 06723-2540

Tennesee State Blacksmith & Farrier School
3780 Shepardsville Hwy.
Bloomington Springs, TN 38545

Tennessee State University
Nashville, TN 37209-1561

Texas A&M University
Department of Animal Science
College Station, TX 77843

Texas Horseshoeing School
Box 188
Scurry, TX 75158

Texas State Horseshoeing School
4407 Precinct Road
Weatherford, TX 76086

Texas Tech University
Animal Science Department
P.O. Box 4169
Lubbock, TX 79409

The Fort Valley State College
Fort Valley, GA 31030

Tomball College
Veterinary Technology Program
30555 Tomball Parkway
Tomball, TX 77375-4036

Tri-County Technical College
Equine Studies
Pendleton, SC 29670

Tucson School of Horseshoeing
2230 N. Kimberlee Rd.
Tucson, AZ 85749

Tucumcari Farrier Technologies
Box 36
Tucumcari, NM 88401

Tufts University
College of Veterinary Medicine
200 Westboro Rd.
North Grafton, MA 01536

Tuskegee University
College of Veterinary Medicine
Tuskegee, AL 36088

Tuskegee University
Tuskegee, AL 36088

University of Alaska
Fairbanks, AK 99775-5200

University of Arizona
Animal Sciences Department
4101 N. Campbell Ave.
Tuscon, AZ 85721

University of Arkansas
Little Rock, AR 72203

University of Arkansas
Pine Bluff, AR 71601

University of California–Davis
Animal Science Department
Mark Hall 175
Davis, CA 95616

University of California–Oakland
Oakland, CA 94612-3560

University of Connecticut
Animal Science Department
3636 Horsebarn Rd. Ext.
Box U-40
Storrs, CT 06269-4040

University of Delaware
Department of Animal Science
Newark, DE 19717-1303

The University of Findlay
Center for Equine and Pre-Vet Studies
1000 North Main Street
Findlay, OH 45840

University of Florida
Animal Science Department
106 Animal Science Building
Gainesville, FL 32611

University of Georgia
Livestock-Poultry Building
Athens, GA 30602

University of Guelph
Ontario Veterinary College
Guelph, Ontario N1G 1W1
Canada

University of Hawaii
Honolulu, HI 96822

University of Idaho
Animal Science Department
Moscow, ID 83843

University of Illinois
Department of Animal Science
Champaign-Urbana, IL 61801

University of Kentucky
Department of Animal Science
Lexington, KY 40506

University of Louisville
Department of Equine Administration
School of Business and Public Administration
Louisville, KY 40292

University of Maine–Orono
Department of Animal, Veterinary & Aquatic Science
5735 Hitchner Hall
Orono, ME 04469

University of Maryland
Animal Science Department
P.O. Box 295
College Park, MD 20742

University of Maryland
Eastern Shore, MD 21853

University of Massachusetts
Department of Animal Science
317 Stockbridge Hall
Amherst, MA 01003

University of Minnesota
College of Veterinary Medicine
St. Paul, MN 55108

University of Minnesota–Crookston
Ag. Management Division
109 Hill Hall
Crookston, MN 56716-5001

University of Missouri–Columbia
Department of Animal Science
Columbia, MO 65211

University of Nebraska
Lincoln, NE 68583-0703

University of Nevada
School of Veterinary Medicine
Reno, NV 89557-0104

University of New Hampshire
Department of Animal Science
Kendall Hall
Durham, NH 03824

University of Pennsylvania
College of Veterinary Medicine
3800 Spruce Street
Philadelphia, PA 19104

University of Rhode Island
Reckham Animal Center
Kingston, RI 02881-0804

University of Saskatchewan
Western College of Veterinary Medicine
Saskatoon, Saskatchewan S7N 0W0
Canada

University of Tennessee
Department of Animal Science
305 Student Services Building
Knoxville, TN 37996

University of the District of Columbia
Washington, DC 20008

University of Vermont
Equine Sciences
212 Terrill Hall
Burlington, VT 05405

Unversity of Wisconsin - Madison
College of Veterinary Medicine
Madison, WI 53706

University of Wisconsin–River Falls
Animal Science Department
River Falls, WI 54022

University of Wyoming
Laramie, WY 82071

Utah State University
Department of Animal Science
Logan, UT 84322-4900

Vermont Technical College
Veterinary Technology Program
Randolph Center, VT 05061

Virgina Intermont College
1013 Moore Street
Campus Box D460
Bristol, VA 24201

Virginia Highlands Community College
Equine Studies
P.O. Box 828
Abingdon, VA 24212-0828

Virginia Polytechnic Institute
  & State University
Animal and Poultry Department
Blacksburg, VA 24061-0306

Virginia State University
Petersburg, VA 23803

Virginia-Maryland Regional College
  of Veterinary Medicine
Blacksburg, VA 24061-0442

Walla Walla Community College
500 Tausick Way
WallaWalla, WA 99362

Washington State University
Department of Animal Science
Pullman, WA 99164-6310

Wayne County Community College
Veterinary Technology Program
540 E. Canfield
Detroit, MI 48201

West Texas State University
Box 998 West Texas Station
Department of Animal Science
Canyon, TX 79016

West Virginia University
Morgantown, WV 26506

Western Kentucky University
College of Agriculture
Bowling Green, KY 42101

Western Nevada Community College
2201 West Nye Lane
Carson City, NV 89703

Western Wyoming Community College
Equine Studies
2500 College Drive
P.O. Box 428
Rock Springs, WY 82902

Western's School of Horseshoeing
2801 W. Maryland Ave.
Phoenix, AZ 85017

White Wood Farm Equestrian Training Center
90 Route 80
Killingworth, CT 06419

William Woods College
Equestrian Science Department
200 W. Twelfth St.
Fulton, MO 65251

Willmar Technical College
Veterinary Technology Department
2101 15th Ave. NW
Willmar, MN 56201

Wilson College
Equine Studies
1015 Philadelphia Avenue
Chambersburg, PA 17201

Wolverine Farrier School
7690 Wiggins Rd.
Howell, MI 48843

Wood Junior College
Equine Studies
P.O. Drawer C
Mathiston, MS 39752

Woodcock Hill Riding Academy
Willington, CT 06279

World Wide College of Auctioneering Inc.
P.O. Box 949
Mason City, IA 50402-0949

Yuba College
Animal Health Technology Program
2088 N. Beale Rd.
Marysville, CA 9590

SELECTED EQUINE SPORT ASSOCIATIONS

American Driving Society
P.O. Box 160
Metamora, MI 48455-0160

American Horse Shows Association, Inc.
220 E. 42nd Street—#409
New York, NY 10017-5876

American Quarter Horse Association
P.O. Box 200
Amarillo, TX 79168-0001

National Cutting Horse Association
4704 Hwy 377 South
Augusta, GA 30901-1305

National Reining Horse Association
448 Main St— #204
Coshocton, OH 43812-1200

National Steeplechase Association
400 Fair Hill Drive
Elkton, MD 21921-2569

Professional Rodeo Cowboys Association
101 Pro Rodeo Drive
Colorado Springs, CO 80919-998

United States Combined Driving Association
P.O. Box 2247
Leesburg, VA 22075-2247

United States Dressage Federation
P.O. Box 6669
Lincoln, NE 68506-0669

United States Equestrian Team
Pottersville Rd.
Gladstone, NJ 07934

United States Polo Association
4059 Iron Works Pike
Lexington, KY 40511-8434

The 25 Largest Breed Associations

American Hackney Horse Society
4059 Iron Works Pike #A
Lexington, KY 40511-8462

American Miniature Horse Association
2908 SE Loop 820
Fort Worth, TX 76140-1073

American Morgan Horse Association
P.O. Box 960
Shelburne, VT 05482-0960

American Paint Horse Association
P.O. Box 961023
Fort Worth, TX 76161-0023

American Quarter Horse Association
P.O. Box 200
Amarillo, TX 79168

American Saddlebred Horse Association
4093 Iron Works Pike
Lexington, KY 40511-8434

American Shetland Pony Club
P.O. Box 3415
Peoria, IL 61614-3415

Appaloosa Horse Club, Inc.
P.O. Box 8403
Moscow, ID 83843-0903

Arabian Horse Registry of America
12000 Zuni St.
Westminster, CO 80234-2300

International Arabian Horse Association—
   Half-Arabian and Anglo-Arabian Registries
P.O. Box 33696
Denver, CO 80233-0696

International Buckskin Horse Association
P.O. Box 268
Shelby, IN 46377-0268

International Trotting and Pacing Assoc (Trottingbred)
575 Broadway
Hanover, PA 17331-2007

The Jockey Club (Thoroughbred)
821 Corporate Drive
Lexington, KY 40503-2794

Missouri Fox Trotting Horse Breed Association
P.O. Box 1027
Ava, MO 65608-1027

National Show Horse Registry
11700 Commonwealth Drive
Suite #200
Louisville, KY 40299-2344

Palomino Horse Breeders of America
15253 E. Skelly Drive
Tulsa, OK 74116-2637

Paso Fino Horse Association
100 W. Main
P.O. Box 600
Bowling Green, FL 33834-0600

Percheron Horse Association of America
P.O. Box 141
Fredericktown, OH 43019-0141

Peruvian Paso Horse Registry of North America
1038 4th Street #4
Santa Rosa, CA 95404-4319

Pinto Horse Association of America
1900 Samuels Avenue
Fort Worth, TX 76102-1141

Pony of The Americas Club, Incorporated
5240 Elmwood Ave.
Indianapolis, IN 46203-5990

Racking Horse Breeders Association of America
Rt. 2 Box 72-A
Decatur, AL 35603

Tennessee Walking Horse Breeders and
   Exhibitors Association
P.O. Box 286
Lewisburg, TN 37091-0286

United States Trotting Association (Standardbred)
750 Michigan Ave.
Columbus, OH 43215-1191

Welsh Pony & Cob Society of America
P.O. Box 2977
Winchester, VA 22604-2977

REGIONAL HORSE DIRECTORIES

Alaska Horse Directory
4122 Hook Ct.
Anchorage, AK 99517

*All About Horses: A Complete Directory for the
New Jersey Equine Industry*
1321 Washington Street
Hoboken, NJ 07030

The Arizona Horse Pages
P.O. Box 31758
Phoenix, AZ 85046-1758

California Horseman's Directory
3790 Via de la Valle #204 #277
Del Mar, CA 92014

Horse Central Directory (East Tennessee)
P.O. Box 5600
Cleveland, TN 37320-5600

Horseman's Yellow Pages (Northern California)
P.O. Box 2571
Kirkland, WA 98083-2571

Imagine—The Horse Source (Rocky Mountains)
P.O. Box 376
Oregon, IL 61061-0376

Just Horses: A Directory for Connecticut
P.O. Box 10
Huntington, MA 01050-0010

Midwest Horseman's Directory
8407 Regnier Rd.
Hebron, IL 60034

Missouri Equine Council Horse Industry Directory
Rt. 1 Box 215
Brookline, MO 65619-9794

Northwest Horseman's Directory
P.O. Box 2571
Kirkland, WA 98083-2571

Oregon Horseman's Directory
P.O. Box 2571
Kirkland, WA 98083-2571

State of Colorado Horseman's Yellow Pages
P.O. Box 2571
Kirkland, WA 98083-2571

Suburban Horseman (Maryland and Virginia)
P.O. Box 3369
Reston, VA 22090-3369

Texas Horseman's Directory
P.O. Box 625
Cypress, TX 77429

Vermont Horse Council Equine Directory
RR. #1 Box 398
Williamstown, VT 05679

Virginia Horse Council Horse Industry Directory
2178 Mt.Tabor Road
Blacksburg, VA 24060

Index